Blue & White dynamite

IAN DURRANT
with
IAIN KING

FIRST PRESS
PUBLISHING

Blue & White Dynamite

Published by First Press Publishing Limited
193-197 Bath Street, Glasgow G2 4HU
© First Press Publishing Limited

ISBN 1 901603 075

Printed and bound in Scotland

Contents

*THIS book is especially dedicated to two special ladies -
Ruby Durrant and Leila King - from two mammy's boys.
And also, of course, to our wives Angela and Lorna for
putting up with us as we put it together.*

IAN DURRANT and IAIN KING, April 1998

FOREWORD
By ALLY McCOIST MBE

I HAVE made many friends in this football life, but in Ian Durrant I found the little brother I never had.

That's how I introduce him to people. And I mean it from the heart.

It's not false sentiment. Ian has been with me when I've been hitting the heights in football and he's been with me when I've been at my depths away from the limelight that has shone on us these last 15 years.

Everyone knows the legend of McCoist and Durrant, the Rangers fans who grew up to play for the team, win a sackful of medals and have a million laughs along the way.

We have been lucky boys.

We have success, lovely wives and families. We have health, wealth and happiness even though our Ibrox days are now drawing to a close. Yet the most precious trophy of all from our Gers days is each other and we will be friends until the day we die.

Ian is a totally different character from me, a quieter personality in public but in the dressing-room he's the King of the one-liners, the acid wit who can cut you to ribbons.

Thirteen years on if I'm ever winning an argument he will *always* chirp back and tell me that when I scored a hat-trick in a 3-0 win over Morton on his debut it said **DURRANT** on the Man of the Match trophy.

He's never let me forget that - and don't tell him, but to be honest even I couldn't complain that day. He was brilliant and his performance was the shape of things to come.

I would do anything for Ian ... he is even the one man I'd ever dream of getting into a fight for. I protected him in my hometown of East Kilbride back in 1986 and it was **ME** who walked out of court convicted!

I'm not proud of that night. Having a criminal record is humiliating.

But even then we could find some black humour in a serious and embarrassing situation as we sat together in an interrogation room at the cop shop.

We were bored and a big, bluff sergeant walked in to find us playing shove ha'penny on the table. He wasn't too impressed.

I started to panic when he sat down grumpily, stared across at me and asked: "Do you have a police record, Mr McCoist?"

Quick as a flash, Durrant pipes up: "Aye, Walking on the Moon."

That really helped my case!

That was Durranty and this is a book which tells you so much more about the **REAL** guy, a footballer I've been proud to play beside and a man I'm proud to call a mate. God knows, I never always saw eye-to-eye with Graeme Souness but he was right when he said the likes of Juventus or AC Milan would have taken Ian to Italy if he hadn't been so badly injured.

He was **THE** *player of his generation.*

Never underestimate what we lost the day he went down under the force of that infamous Neil Simpson tackle at Aberdeen.

And never underestimate the courage and willpower it has taken to fight back from **SEVEN** heartbreaking operations. Lesser men - yes, myself included - would have chucked it.

Ian is a funny man. But chip away at his veneer and you find someone with desire, will to win and an incredibly strong heart.

To be back playing at all, at any level, is a testament to the character of Ian Durrant. He would have done well to get back to play in a **PUB** league - yet he came back and played in the **CHAMPIONS** League.

And he did that because of what beats within him. You can get all the specialist help in the world, all the docs and all the physios but at the end of the day when you have an injury like his it comes down to one person and one person only.

Yourself.

Ian went through mental torture to end 30 months out of the game and play again for Rangers and he still fights that battle every minute of every session in the gym.

I watch him bite back tears as he goes through the manipulation his knee needs to get it in shape for another day at the office.

I watch the punishing weights routine he must go through to keep building up the other muscles in his leg to compensate for the damage done a decade ago.

I watch and I think how magnificent he was **AFTER** the injury when he starred in that Champions League run of 1993. And you can only marvel at what a player he was **BEFORE** that fateful split second at 3.08pm on October 8, 1988.

Durranty is a unique footballer because 50 per cent of the game is played in his head. He thinks light years more quickly than average players, his thoughts do more damage than their runs.

His imagination takes him into gaps other midfielders don't see and he makes runs off the ball you simply cannot coach. That's what made him such a precious commodity and that's why he was - and still is - a phenomenal player.

As we sat writing this foreword over lunch, I was challenged to think of my five favourite Durrant goals. So many images cluttered my mind, so many memories. But when I sorted it out you were looking at a real masterclass for midfielders.

From his crashing left foot finish on his European debut against Borussia Monchengladbach to the ghosting run on Davie Cooper's blind side that let him take the pass of his dreams and beat Celtic in 1986.

From a magical 1-2 with me and a cool-as-you-like finish with the outside of his right boot in the 1987 Skol Cup Final against Aberdeen, to the sweeping shot after switching Trevor Steven's pass from left foot to right against Bruges in the Champions League.

And who can forget **THE** Durrant moment, that unbelievable drilled shot in Marseille that swerved into the far corner past Fabien Barthez and so nearly took us to the European Cup Final.

A great player, then, but also a great joker and a man I have had so much fun with through the years.

The laughs never stopped, even when we were injured and sent down to recover together at Lilleshall. Now Graeme Souness and Walter Smith are shrewd - but what were they thinking of back then?

I can't dream up worse people to be in rehab together than Durrant, McCoist and big Norman Whiteside. It's like sending Oliver Reed and Dean Martin to the Betty Ford Clinic together on a curer.

Grant Downie, now at Ibrox, was then the physio at Lilleshall and he will tell you how hard we worked during the day ... but I have to admit we played hard, too.

You were supposed to be under curfew at night but I'll never forget the sight of those three bike lights weaving down the lane in the darkness to the Fox & Duck to see old Ivor the landlord. We had some laughs.

Of course, there has to be discipline and at Ibrox it's a tight ship at times with Archie Knox.

Mind you, he wasn't too impressed on his first club R & R trip when he saw the terracing heroes at their hotel suite window in their boxers saluting him after they'd drank the place out of champagne.

We had gone to St Andrews for one of those famous Rangers "bonding sessions" soon after the Gaffer brought Archie up from Manchester United. We were great believers in working hard and playing hard.

So we got tore in and suddenly they were out of Bollinger. Poor show. Next went the Moet and Chandon and then we moved on to Dom Perignon.

Not bad plonk for two wee boys from East Kilbride and Kinning Park!

But the next day's team meeting was one of the most embarrassing of my Ibrox life. We had been free to go off the leash after a punishing spell chasing trophies, but we'd perhaps gone over the score a little.

Walter Smith's face was grim as he brandished the room extras' bills and he stood there reading them out like a summons: "John Brown £45...Nigel Spackman £62...Stuart McCall £71" The eyebrows arched up at this and I thought: "Disgraceful, McCall's in trouble."

Then he sighed and looked at the two sorry sights in front of him: "McCoist and Durrant £1,262. Explanation?"

To this day Walter has never believed us that the other boys took advantage of the fact we were smashed to put all their bills on our room, but even he smirked in the end.

I've roomed with Durranty all over the world and I laughed my socks off in the Toronto Hilton when we got there for the Canadian dinner in my Testimonial Year.

I'm telling him that as guest of honour I have the best suite in the hotel and he should come and share with me.

So we're slagging all the boys about their pokey double rooms and sure enough when we get up there it's absolutely palatial.

There's a massive four-poster for me and I'm well impressed. Then Durranty sees this little annexe off my room and yelps: "This is mine."

Round he scurries to find his kip - a fold-down **CAMP-BED**!

I was in charge then, as I expect Durranty to be on the Canadian leg of his Testimonial Tour this summer and the rules were: Rendezvous in the McCoist and Durrant suite at 10am with a can of beer in your hand.

You were fined $10 for every half hour you were late! Great days.

We've had a lot of fun together and I think that's why we have such a special bond with the Rangers fans. They know if we weren't players we'd be sitting in the stand shouting the team on. We're living out our boyhood dreams and theirs.

In fact, our lives have always mirrored each others.

We've got each other through the loss of our dads. Played in Cup Finals, scored together. Had a football lifetime with Rangers and had our testimonials too.

We even became fathers at the same time and Ian's son Max and my boy Alexander will grow up together.

Through it all, first and foremost, I have always looked upon Ian as one of my closest pals, a man I have turned to in my darkest hours.

Within the space of two awful weeks in June 1994 I lost my dad Neil and my Uncle George who I was very close to. When you have a privileged and lucky life like mine then you never think bad things can happen to you. I was floored by their deaths, devastated.

There were buckets of tears and when I needed someone to help me I had Durranty. He was there for me, just as I had been when his old man Hughie died.

I can still see us sitting there in his mum Ruby's sitting room and he was at his lowest ebb. I hope I helped him then because I know when I needed someone to cope with my grief I had Ian.

I think it takes a special person in your life to become as close as brothers, I found two in Durranty and Davie Cooper.

I still can't believe Coop is dead. I sat around that hospital after his brain haemorrhage and I just couldn't take it in that he was gone. I mean, why? Why?

Those questions of why a man who meant so much to Ian and I was ripped away before he was 40 can never be answered. But at least we still had each other and when I fell to pieces, Ian played a big role in being strong himself and putting me back together again.

Our friendship has meant a lot to me. At football clubs, players come and go and you laugh and joke with them, score goals and fall out with them. The bottom line is that they are acquaintances, guys you work with until they move onto another club.

But the bond between Ian Durrant and I will go beyond that and beyond the date when we have to leave our beloved Rangers, which is all too fast approaching.

I have a friend for life.

CHAPTER 1

BLUE FOR YOU

IAN DURRANT was born to play for Rangers.
A football-daft kid brought up in the shadow of Ibrox, he was steeped in the club's history from the day he could walk.

Yet when his dreams came true and he signed for his boyhood heroes he joined a club on the slide.

Rangers were lavishing cash on a new-look stadium, the home the fans can be proud of today.

But back then there was a steep price to pay for that vision - the team was suffering badly.

The kid who swapped the terracing for the Ibrox dressing-room was to learn just what Rangers means to the people who follow the club.

And those early times brought some dark days that would be in stark contrast to the career to come...

I SAW the gap, I sneaked through and I was in the clear. Goal for Rangers!

I've always had an eye for an opening. Even when it was in a fence.

And this isn't the story of my Ibrox debut, it's the tale of how I first shared in the joy of a goal for the team I love.

These days I purr up to the front door of Ibrox in a flash Mercedes...but I've never forgotten how I once skipped in the **BACK** way with my pals.

I was nine years old and where I lived in Kinning Park everything revolved around the Rangers.

So we were delighted when we sniffed out a sneaky route to see heroes like John Greig and Tommy McLean without paying a penny.

Over the railway line at the back of the old Centenary Stand - remember that? - and there you were at a fence with a hole just enough for a wee fella like me to squeeze through.

I first broke in on November 29, 1975 and I was hooked. The crowd that day was only 16,500 for a league game with Dundee...but it felt like the World Cup Final to me.

Martin Henderson scored twice, we won 2-1 and I couldn't wait for the next match. For three games we pulled the same dodge. Security wasn't the best back then.

I was there when we beat Ayr 3-0 when big Martin hit the net again, just as he did the following Saturday in a Ibrox win over Motherwell. The memories are still so clear of a big centre-forward who would later be my first Rangers room-mate.

Derek Johnstone scored twice against a Well side that had hard men like Willie McVie in it. DJ is a true Rangers great who remains a great pal to this day - despite working for Radio Clyde!

Those guys were my heroes, from Greigy at the back to DJ and Derek Parlane up front. Parlane was the glamour boy then - I'd stand on the terraces belting out: "Parlane, Parlane, born is the King of Ibrox".

And I still give that the full treatment at nostalgia nights in my old local, The District Bar.

I come from a Rangers heartland, just like Alex MacDonald who was also born and bred in Kinning Park. If I wanted to see how far you could go I just looked at the little redhead in the No.6 shirt.

Who would have believed that one day I would wear that same shirt on my first team debut?

Watching those stars when you could only dream of the money to pay in meant the world - so when they boarded the hole up I was distraught.

The fact that our personal boys' gate disappeared before the Ne'erday Old Firm game made it a hundred times worse.

We had met up as usual outside my house in Craigiehall Street and set off for Ibrox talking about hammering the 'Tic. Then we spied the new wood over our gap. We couldn't get through our secret entry. They'd found us out and my heart sank.

We couldn't even get a lift over the turnstiles - the other way to get in free in those days - because admission was tighter for Old Firm games. So we stood outside and listened to the noise, trying to guess what was happening inside - and waited for 20 minutes to go when they opened the gates and we finally got in for nothing.

We still savoured some of a 1-0 win earned by a DJ goal without shelling out a penny. Not something you can imagine happening in these days of Sky TV and corporate hospitality!

After that early setback, though, I just seemed to have the sort of face people felt sorry for and I'd still get lifted over most weeks.

Years later Greigy and wee Tam would be my bosses at the club but I never told them about my free ticket to the game - they'd have docked my wages!

When I first watched Rangers they were the bosses in Scottish football, a team who who would win two Trebles in three seasons.

Every kid in my street wanted to pull on the jersey and I couldn't play enough football as I tried to make it something more than just a dream.

Rangers strips were prized in our house and I always got my brother's cast-offs. The first was the famous blue jersey with the white V neck and that great badge that covered half your chest!

I loved that strip, even if it was a far cry from today when you see kids cutting around in the full Nike kit. I wore any old shorts and socks, just as long as I had the jersey.

With my latest Gers top guaranteed once it no longer fitted big brother, I always got my other favourite at Christmas, the Liverpool top. Kenny Dalglish was - and still is - my hero.

I was out with Hitachi plastered across my chest - whether it was the red top or my favourite white change one - day after day, running around pretending to be King Kenny.

I couldn't afford to get No.7 stuck on the back, but I knew in my mind that I was Dalglish.

Luxury was flicking the Mouldmaster from foot to foot then crashing one past a keeper on our local black ash pitches. Ninety minutes out there and you looked as if you'd done a double shift down the mines.

There was no point in a leather bladder on that surface, it would only have been ruined - and when the Mouldmaster burst we moved down to a tennis ball. I honed my control using one of those - kids today hone theirs on a Playstation.

Back then my interests were simpler. I was a member of the 99th Boys' Brigade in Kinning Park with my brothers Alan - who'd grow up to be a silky midfielder - and James, the mauler of the family!

16

Alan spent a year at East Stirling but went back to be a top amateur player with Coatbridge CC and James - the Durrants had to have one defender - is now coaching with Renfrew Juniors. Football ruled in our family, so it wasn't much fun for my sister Ann. I'll always remember Alan and I having a strike partnership up front for a team called Malvern Star. I scored all the goals, he took all the credit.

While we loved the BB for the discipline and a feeling of belonging that it gave us, it helped that they had a football team.

I'd play with them on the Saturday morning before moving on to my youth side Glasgow United in the afternoon.

We played at a sprawling complex called the 50 Pitches - not far from Ibrox - and if we played in the Scottish Cup against a team from Ayrshire or Aberdeen who were used to grass they were soon picking red gravel out of their legs.

We'd relish drawing them at their patch, though, because it meant that rare chance to play on grass and give your screw-ins their only outing of the year. Unless you reached a final, of course.

Miller Hay, my gym teacher at Bellahouston Academy, was playing a key role in rearing me and even then I'd daydream I was Dalglish. King Kenny had grown up just along the road from me and lived in the Ibrox high flats. It's always bugged me that he got through the net and never joined Rangers.

When I was playing until dark as a kid I'd never have dreamed that one day I'd play beside the great man himself.

My big day came in 1990 in a bounce game at Troon organised by Graeme Souness. Glasgow had been frostbound and we needed match practice, so this game was set up. And to my amazement, when we turned up Kenny - up for a break with his old Liverpool and Scotland pal who was now our boss - was there. He came on in the last 20 minutes and we played up front together as our Whites beat the Blues 4-3 at humble Portland Park.

Kenny didn't score, but although he was 38 then all the touches were still there. He was as brilliant as ever.

I was awestruck then and I am now. Like every player, he gets stuck with a silly nickname - but when I opened my mouth to shout "Dalgy" I kept stuttering.

At the end, he came over and wished me well in recovering from my injury and wandered off. We've spoken since and it gets a *little* easier, but almost every time I am lost for words, I muck up the conversation.

Still, I'll quit knowing I met and played with my hero and I couldn't have imagined that when a scout called Archie Lawrie first spotted me.

I was 13 and had only just restarted playing after - you've guessed it - an injury. My mum and dad had scrimped and saved to send me to Italy

17

skiing with the school for two days. It was 1980, the first trip abroad of my life and I rewarded them by returning home with a broken leg.

I had all the gear, the best we could manage, but I slithered into a bit of bother out on the piste.

So I wasn't long back from that setback when I made the short journey to Ibrox as a player for the first time. The place has been my life ever since. Sure, at first I was just this skinny kid coming to the club he loved twice a week for coaching.

But I could always pray for Easter because that brought the holidays and the chance that you might get an opportunity to meet - and even train beside - some of the first-team players.

I must have shown some promise because soon enough I was signed as an apprentice under Davie Provan, Stan Anderson and Joe Mason.

There was no real youth team then. We were just pulled together at times to represent the club abroad. Quite often you'd be hauled into first-team training and even then, in those troubled days John Greig had as boss, you could see how good a coach Tommy McLean was.

In the afternoons, Tam would put a squad of us through our paces. Derek Ferguson, Hugh Burns, Davie McFarlane, Robert Fleck and I were all pushing for the first team and he knew how to make you listen.

Everything was geared towards improving you as a player. We still trained at the old Albion then and Tam had great methods that sound so simple, yet were very effective.

Running was off the menu. It was all football. There were big boards and he'd drill you to stand there judging the pace of pass back and forth. Then you'd go through the gears and start rapping the ball at pace with both feet to test your touch.

It was a throwback to my youth when I used to practice in Blackburn Street - only to see my programme cut short when I smashed a window in Gall's the wool shop and scarpered. In fact, I did that a few times - the owner's probably due a slice of my pension if he ever finds out.

Coaches like Tommy made sure I kept learning and the family were happy about that because my dad Hugh had first-hand knowledge that football was the **ONLY** thing I would be any good at.

He was a scaffolder and when apprentice wages dropped in the summer I went to work for him. But you know how it is - I was always mucking around and playing on the forklifts and he sacked me after a month!

Shipbuilding was the big industry in Kinning Park when I was a kid, but I was lucky enough to find a better way.

It was a real close-knit place, so much so that even now I've moved away I still go back. When I was young my mum had so many friends I had 40 "aunties" whose back doors I could nip into for something to eat.

I still see them all and while they might admire whatever car I have at the time they always remember I was the first person in my family to actually pass their driving test.

The trappings of my success back then? A very dodgy red Ford Capri with a flash down it that looked like a prop from Starsky and Hutch. With furry dice, of course!

Any time I'm home for a pint or to watch pub football tournaments and get a bit lippy they remind me of a car that became known as the Red Devil.

I loved that car, yet it had a petrol gauge that didn't work, so you never knew if it was full or empty. The inevitable happened when my brother-in-law took it out one day and ran out of juice.

He parked it under a light for safety - and somebody ran into the back and wrecked it. A tragedy.

Even today, everyone at home has plenty ammunition on me if I start firing the crack - they bring up the infamous Red Devil.

I like it when they bite back because I would never decry the people or the place where I came from. It means a lot that people see me alongside the likes of Alex MacDonald and Kenny Dalglish.

We should be role models especially when there's a lovely, big red ash pitch in the middle of the estate now. Yet when I go back there are no kids on the corner kicking a can under the streetlights because they haven't got a ball like I used to.

They're all inside playing their computers which is sad because it shows I'm getting old! When I was their age life was simple because I knew where I wanted to be. Ibrox.

I'd signed a form to commit myself to Rangers and I was allowed to leave Bellahouston Academy at 15-and-a-half to take my chances.

I was on my way, but those were depressing days for the Gers, times when you knew things couldn't really change quickly because all the money was being pumped into rebuilding the stadium. None of it was going on players.

I felt sorry for John Greig because he had so much to live up to as a boss after his playing career. His nickname at the club is Ledge - short for Legend - and that sums up a guy who led the club to those Trebles and lifted the Cup-Winners' Cup in 1972.

I was just a kid when John was in trouble in the hotseat, but you get to learn about situations as a player. A new manager comes in and he wants to change things but there's a big squad on good wages and they don't want to go.

As we wrote this book Alex McLeish faced the very same problems at Hibs and it reminded me of Greigy. He was trying to cut a large staff but there were discontented players in there and that filtered through on to the park.

There was a bad atmosphere hanging around the halls and even as a groundstaff boy I could detect it. It all peaked one awful day at Ibrox in October 1983 when we lost 2-1 to Motherwell in front of a half-empty stadium and I stood behind the dugout watching in disbelief.

The fans hurled scarves onto the park - those fans who were left, that is. By the end we were down to the diehards. Rangers were in a sorry state.

Everything welled up in the supporters that day, the success of clubs like Aberdeen, Dundee United and Celtic while they were sitting in a beautiful ground watching a bad team.

One of my jobs in the aftermath of a game that would cost John his job was to walk along the track picking up discarded scarves. It hurt inside.

There was an eerie feel to the dressing-room when I paid a brief visit to pick up the boots for cleaning, a chill which has stayed with me. It was the end of something, you could sense it.

I watched Greigy have it so hard as manager that eventually he was battering his head against a brick wall. It hurt and saddened me when he left because I'd been honoured to simply be around a heart-and-soul Rangers man like him.

Yet in later years I would look back and think that getting out when he did made Greigy a better and happier person.

Me? It had only been when Derek Ferguson and I were taken to Porto as hamper boys for a European tie that I started to think they might rate me. It poured with rain that night and we lost 1-0 to go out on away goals after Sandy Clark and Davie Mitchell scored in a 2-1 home win.

Working as the boot-boy on trips like that meant a lot of menial tasks, but it was a swift business trip in those days. There was no loosen-up training session on matchday as there is now, just lunch then a light pre-match meal before heading for the ground.

I listened and learned and even just that involvement on the fringes made me think I might be going places.

With Jock Wallace succeeding Greigy, I knew for sure when we went to a youth tournament in Dusseldorf that he was watching me closely. In the end that competition **MADE** me as a Rangers player.

We had a lot of good youngsters in that side with Burns, Fleck and Fergie joined by the likes of John Davies and an Icelandic kid called Siggi Jonsson. Siggi has ended up at Dundee United after a lot of injuries, but back then he had everyone in Britain chasing him and he eventually opted for Arsenal in front of us.

With players like those you can see we had the quality to do well. I had a stormer and ended up top goalscorer. By the time we came back I was walking on air, Jock offered me a three-year deal deal and I bit his hand off. I'd made it.

In these days of £25,000-a-week players you'd laugh at my first

Rangers contract. I was on £70 a week but Jock gave me £800 extra to sign and I thought I'd won the pools.

My wages would rise to £300 if I was in the first-team with £100 appearance cash and £120 win bonus.

The best of weeks meant £520 and I couldn't believe money like that - my entire **FAMILY** weren't making that at the time.

But cash has never really been what it is all about for me.

As you get older you learn to look after yourself in these negotiations, but back then all I wanted to do was play for the first team.

And when I made it, one woman wouldn't have missed it for the world. My mum Ruby.

She's always been my biggest influence. She has seen **EVERY** game I've played in since I was eight years old. From the reserves at Pittodrie to the handful of matches on loan with Everton, she's been there for me.

And later when I was so badly injured it was mum who was there to help me through the nightmare spells when I felt the whole world was against me.

I was down at Lilleshall, trudging along the long road to recovery in 1989 when I got the call every son dreads. My dad was dead.

A massive heart attack had taken him away and it cuts me to the quick that he never saw me make my comeback.

We were close and it floored me. I couldn't handle it, but again I drew strength from my mum. Despite her own grief she dragged me back up and I stayed at her house for about six months.

I'll never forget what she did for me back then.

So as I look back on this career at Rangers it's with pride that Hugh and Ruby Durrant saw their youngest son in the light blue.

The biggest day of my life arrived on April 2, 1985. I was 18 and fresh from a stormer in a 3-1 reserve win over St Johnstone at Ibrox. Still, there was no real indication that promotion was ahead until the Friday when Alex Totten told me to train with the first team.

The reserves trained on one half of the Albion pitch with the first team at the end that counts.

I ripped through the warm-up, the five-a-sides and was on a scoring streak as we practiced crossing and finishing. I was really buzzing, but still no word.

At the end of the session I started the walk back to the park with my ball under my arm. That sounds odd now, but Jock had standards - there were no tracksuit bottoms for training, just shorts and your socks had to be kept up with tie-ups. Always.

You also carried your own ball back and forth from the training pitch, so there I was walking back when big Jock suddenly appeared behind me and said: "How are you feeling? Are you up for it tomorrow?"

The ten words I had waited for all my life.

We took off our boots at the oak doors of the famous marble hall at the entrance to Ibrox. From there, I would normally have turned right towards the reserve dressing-room deep in the bowels of the stadium.

This time, Totty told me to veer left towards the hallowed first-team room because Jock was naming the side for the trip to Cappielow. There at No.6 was the name of Durrant, in a midfield with Robert Prytz in the centre and Cammy Fraser on the right.

I plucked up the bottle to ask for three extra tickets for my family to add to the two comps we are always issued and Jock got me them.

It was a lovely day for us and I know my dad was proud, even though he never kicked his own backside as a footballer. My mum must have been the player in our family.

The good thing is Dad passed on the slight frame that's kept me naturally fit throughout my career. He was like me, a guy who enjoyed his banter but had his quiet side. I think that is how anyone who *really* knows would describe me.

When I look back, he was always there for me and my son Max will grow up knowing he'll get the same from me.

I relished every second of my debut day. When I think back now there were no real nerves, just this feeling that I was meant to be there.

That's not arrogance. It's just that I felt this was all I'd ever worked for and even if that game against Morton was my **LAST** for Rangers I was going to savour it all.

In the end we won 3-0, Ally McCoist scored a hat-trick and I was still named Man of the Match. Like he says, I've never let him forget that.

Those were tough times for a team out of contention for a title that would be won by Aberdeen but there were still some good players at the club. I played beside Cammy and Robert in midfield that day but it could have been Michael and Jermaine because I looked like one of the Jackson Five with my mad perm!

Despite the hair, though, I set up one of those goals for McCoist and that was the start of our onfield rapport.

Off it, our friendship had already got off the ground because I was his **BOOT-BOY**. He was a useless boss. He never gave me a bung and he has the smelliest boots in Scottish football, yet we got on so well.

Our lives have been tied together at Rangers and I've seen him at his highest peak and his lowest depths.

That rare nightmare time in the life of Ally McCoist MBE had come earlier that season when we lost 1-0 at home to Dundee in the Scottish Cup. I'll always remember how he kept showing for the ball that day - and he kept missing.

It happens. Even goalscorers like Ally dry up, but he had this courage that drove him on. He refused to hide as more and more abuse piled down from the stands.

John Brown, who would later become a close pal at Rangers, had a stormer for Dundee that day and we went out.

I was still in the reserves then but I sat and watched and listened as the whole crowd bayed: "Ally, Ally - Get tae ****"

The dressing-room afterwards was an emotional place when I went in to do my chores and get the boots. Coisty was in tears.

I felt for him because he had constantly made himself available for the ball and tried to turn things round, but it just didn't come off that day.

There were furious fans waiting outside and he got more than a few bits of advice to go out the side door - but that is not Ally's style, that's not the man he is.

He put his head up and walked out that front door straight into the flak. Mind you, he did have Colin McAdam and Derek Johnstone for company, so at least nobody was going to swing a punch at him!

Through all the doom and gloom at the club I was learning the huge impact Rangers Football Club has on peoples' lives. My pal Davie Currie owns the District Bar and I saw how it affected even him.

He had to make a living yet there were only maybe 8,000 fans turning up in a 40,000 capacity stadium - only those steeped in the club were left.

Through it all, though, I know now how much Ally helped me. He was only 22 yet all the younger players looked up to him.

He has always been The Man in the dressing-room and there were countless times when I'd plead for a run home to Kinning Park so I didn't have to walk in the rain and we'd sit in his car talking football.

It meant a lot because I honestly didn't think I was going to make it at Ibrox. I was very light, 9st and so skinny I had to run around in the showers to get wet. But big Jock saw something there and took a chance on me. The fact that I looked like a skelf in a blue jersey bothered him, though, and soon I would be traipsing up to the kitchen every morning for a bowl of porridge and a pint of milk to fatten me up.

That and the weights regime he had me on worked - within a year I was over half a stone heavier and harder to dispossess. Jock was very fitness orientated and scared me stiff when he stood halfway up the hill at Gullane with a pole in his hand.

If you weren't going up those infamous sands fast enough for his liking you got a helping hand with the pole right up your backside.

There was no namby-pamby crap with Jock, just a man who told you straight where you were going wrong. If you didn't take it on board you knew what would happen next.

We played in Spain against Atletico Osasuna and lost 2-0 to go out of Europe and Derek Ferguson and I were carrying on in our room, little knowing it was next to Jock's.

Before we knew where we were he'd battered through the door and told us to shut up or else. I was shaking. *Shut up*. That was one of his favourite sayings and I always called him Windsor Davies because he was like that Sergeant Major in *It Ain't Half Hot Mum*!

I've always listened to the real Rangers fans to see what they think of people at the club and I don't have to travel far for that. I still go into the District Bar - just up Paisley Road West from the stadium - after games and all my jerseys are on the wall in there which I'm proud of.

They loved Jock in there, from the Glasgow punters to the Irish folk who spend so much money to come over for games.

I grieved when we lost the Big Man in the summer of 1996 and Ally and I were at the funeral. I still recalled the year before when my wife Angela and I met up with Jock and his missus Daphne in Fuengirola.

We had a few drinks, talked about the old days and he told me that I was always **HIS** boy, that he'd made me. I wouldn't argue with that, it touched me he felt that way. He was a colossus and I'll never forget him.

Back in 1986, second-time around at Gers hadn't worked for Jock and there was a revolution coming. I knew from the minute Graeme Souness walked in and told us he only fancied **FIVE** of us that things would change forever at Rangers.

There were even little details about the place he couldn't stomach.

We had these old clothes driers and after training you hung your gear by them and stuck it on again next day. They washed it twice a week but there were times your kit was so stiff with mud it felt like **CARDBOARD**.

For a club with the stature of Rangers the place had fallen behind the times but, believe me, Souness was to change all that.

CHAPTER 2

SOUNESS STORMS IN

RANGERS were in the gutter but Graeme Souness dragged them back to life.

The Souness Revolution brought five years of triumph and turmoil to Ibrox as the club's most controversial manager rampaged through the Scottish game on an unstoppable rescue mission.

Right from the start the new manager saw something special in Ian Durrant, a gift that lifted him beyond the average Scottish player.

They would have feuds and fall-outs but Souness' regard of Durrant the footballer never changed.

This was the kid that he tipped to emulate his own success in Italian football and Ian would relish life at the heart of the storm as the winds of change ripped through Rangers.

He saw the class and the fun, the cruelty and the fury. And he emerged to reflect on the man he believes SAVED Rangers...

IT was 5.15pm on May 2, 1987 - just half an hour after Rangers had won their first title for nine years.

And in seconds I went from singing champion's tunes on the team bus to being fined £1,500 for fighting in a chippy!

That was the day and the moment I found out the true essence of Graeme Souness.

We'd just drawn 1-1 at Pittodrie to clinch the championship at the end of an incredible first season in charge for the new gaffer. Souness himself had been sent off, Terry Butcher had scored to win the point we needed and I'd even survived one of the craziest pitch invasions ever. Our fans had waited so long for that moment they came on wanting souvenirs - **ANY** souvenir.

I dragged myself off the pitch with one boot, a sock and a pair of knickers on. The punters stole the rest but I didn't care. In fact, those manic celebrations seemed to blow away a cloud that had been hanging over me that season.

I'd been in trouble with the law when I got involved in a scrap with a guy in an East Kilbride chip shop. It was a farce. I was out with Ally and Ted McMinn and I was on **CRUTCHES** after an ankle injury.

Ally McCoist saved my life that night, because the fella turned on me in the chippy queue and I wasn't exactly in the best nick to defend myself. Looking back, I was young and naive and I was caught out.

If it happened to me now I would let him have his say and reply: "Fine pal." Then I'd let him walk away.

But when some loudmouth is out to make a name for himself and he starts shouting the odds before trying to assault you, it's in your nature not to just stand there - even on crutches.

My pal Ally jumped in and because of that he has a criminal record which hurts me. It's still a sore point with my mum too. She feels people tried to stitch me up and it affected her badly to see her son in trouble with the law and dragged into court.

I was charged with breach of the peace and assault - both were thrown out. Ally faced the same charges and was eventually convicted of minor assault and fined £150.

It led to a lot of problems for both of us and at one point I even told Souness I would be better off playing my football outside of Glasgow.

I felt trapped. In the wake of East Kilbride, Robert Fleck, John McGregor and I were accused of another fracas in Airdrie on a Thursday night after we'd recorded a single called The Glasgow Rangers Boys at studios in the town.

We shouldn't have been there and Souness cracked up. But a quiet pint turned into a drama - it seemed there would be trouble wherever we went on a night out. We were all fined £1,000 for our part in it. I slapped in a transfer request. Things were going from bad to worse. Ted was so fed-up with the grief he fled to Spain to play for Seville. I always remember after the trial he told me: "When you're a Rangers player, you're a target. Simple as that."

I decided I would have to live with life as a guy up there to be shot at and I made my apology to the Gaffer. In some ways now I reflect on the chippy incident and feel we fell for it.

Some bar-room football genius wanted to make a name for himself and we got caught up in this nonsense. It left my closest friend with a tag he in no way deserves.

Yet the good thing is people remember Ally McCoist MBE, not the other tag he was stuck with for a while after a night out that went wrong.

The court case was troubling that season and there's no question it had an effect on both of us, especially as it happened in Ally's home town.

But now, after all we'd been through together, we were the champions. Our bus was a zoo - and while we were all partying, Souness shouted Coisty and I down to the front.

I'm thinking it's to say thanks but he snaps: "That business in the chip shop, it's not on. You're both fined £1,500.

"Behave yourselves for the next six months and I'll give you it back."

I couldn't believe it...30 minutes earlier we'd won the title and here he was fining us. We got the money back eventually but **THAT** was Souness in a nutshell.

He was hyped up that day for sure. He hadn't been playing regularly but on the Thursday before he was on his toes buzzing at training and I knew he fancied it at Pittodrie.

He always seemed so cool, but although we'd won the League Cup I think he knew he'd be hung, drawn and quartered if he didn't win that first title since 1978.

So, yes, even Mr Cool was on edge that day and it showed on the park. Some of the tackles that flew in were scary and Souness only lasted half an hour before he saw red...**AGAIN!**

Nine months earlier he'd seen red for booting George McCluskey in an opening day defeat from Hibs that became infamous for the 21-man brawl that followed his bust-up.

Now he was off once more and we were right under the cosh for ten minutes before breaking away to win a free-kick. Davie Cooper whipped it in, big Tel rose and we were on our way.

They equalised, but we did it and at least when I finish I'll have one happy memory of Pittodrie to take with me. God knows my nights have been filled with enough nightmares about the place.

That game was the end of a campaign full of the triumphs and tantrums that were to become part of life in Graeme's days at Ibrox.

27

To be honest, I revelled in it all - and I respected him immensely.

Yet my over-riding emotion the day he arrived was sadness because we knew then that Alex Totten and John Hagart, men I respected from Jock Wallace's regime, wouldn't be involved for long. Graeme's first act was to call a critically-important team meeting with his new players.

And McCoist turned up five minutes LATE!

Maybe that was the sign of things to come with them - it certainly gave him a hint of the world-renowned Ally timekeeping. Coisty told me afterwards it was the earliest he'd been late for a while.

For those of us there on time, it was laid on the line right away. There would be big changes. We had five weeks to prove ourselves. Walter Smith was coming in to look after things until Graeme was free from Sampdoria and that was that.

A lot of people knew the writing was on the wall for them. That was the way it would be from then on as he turned the club around, ruthless.

That was Souness the manager, but he was a man I already knew was special in football terms. I remember when I was on Scotland under-21 trips and he was with the big team.

Even in nondescript airport lounges, bustling with people scurrying here and there he seemed to stand out. He had an aura about him. He had presence.

It's hard to describe unless you know these guys, but I used to look at the likes of Souness, Kenny Dalglish and Andy Gray and they all had that same quality that set them apart.

The other thing that set Souness apart, of course, was his temper.

It first bubbled to the surface when we played Bayern Munich in a big pre-season friendly and we were getting hammered. Donald Mackay had come to help out with the coaching and at half-time he was standing by quietly as we got the first Souness riot act.

We had bought Terry and Chris Woods but it wasn't happening yet and the Germans were humiliating us. So Souness is screaming and there's Donald in his brand new suit at his first home game nodding away in agreement.

Graeme eventually lost it, went berserk and slapped this huge great container of orange juice which exploded all over Donald. He wasn't nodding too much after that!

I couldn't laugh because it was **ME** he was shouting at. That 2-0 defeat was my first experience of the legendary Souness fury.

Yet he was such a professional inside the club. He knew football players were creatures of routine who liked to be looked after well so they could give of their best on a Saturday and he transformed the place from the bottom up to make sure it worked that way. There were little things like the day we were all given flip-flops to make sure our feet were protected on the way to the showers. Those added pieces of professionalism sound trivial but they mattered.

Yet he wasn't power-crazy because on the training ground we were dealing mostly with Walter, the best coach I have ever worked under. Souness added the stretching exercises he'd learned in Italy but he knew Walter's class and they were a good mix.

Training changed totally from the way things had been under big Jock. Fitness, fitness and more fitness was the driving factor then, but under Smith you could tell we had a coach who had learned from the best. That's why he went to Mexico 86 with Scotland under Alex Ferguson - Walter understands players and what makes them tick.

There is no gobbledygook or jargon, just drills that make you sharper and better at your job.

Walter would be the first to admit he wasn't an outstanding player, just a steady defender for Dumbarton and Dundee United. But that's why he loves players who **CAN** create, men like Brian Laudrup or Paul Gascoigne. Any system or exercise on the training field he sets up is to free them to play on a Saturday.

Yet, as with Archie Knox under Smith these days, back in 1986 when the players faced the new regime there was no doubt who was in charge right from the off.

Cammy Fraser was out of order at pre-season training in Germany one day and when the rest of us got on the mini-bus, Souness made him **WALK** a mile back to the hotel.

Cammy had been mouthing off all day at training shouting: "You're all ****ing losers...I'm the top man and don't forget it."

We'd had enough so Souness gave the nod from his car and we drove off and left him behind.

There was Fraser chasing behind the mini-bus cursing but there were more problems ahead for the journalist driving us, Graham Clark who is now of the Scottish Express.

Biff, as he's known to everyone in the game because he looks like Biffo Bear out of the Beano, was handling it OK until another bit of nonsense broke out in the back.

We'd often have these rammies on buses. It's really hard to explain to an outsider, but when you're cooped up in a training camp and you're not allowed out there has to be a way to blow off steam.

Sadly for Biff, it happened the day he was driving a grumpy busload of highly-priced footballers down some narrow, twisting country lanes.

We were belting lumps out of each and everyone was punching him and throwing jackets over his head as he drove. He was screaming.

We trooped off back at the hotel with a few of the boys marked and a couple of sure-fire black eyes to come in the morning. Souness looked at

Biff, who'd stopped three times on the way home and was by now chalk-white, and said: "What the **** happened?"

To his credit, Graham remained silent on the incident for the rest of the tour - but he never offered to drive again.

Cammy certainly had his troubles under Souness. One mad training ground punch-up with Hugh Burns sticks in my mind to this day. Cammy had been under the cosh from the fans ever since he flicked a V-sign at them when he was getting abuse and the pressure was on him.

One snide comment was always going to flip him over the edge - he was on tenterhooks. He was walking away on the training park and when Hugh told him he was losing it he suddenly turned.

Sixteen guys split up and Burns and Fraser were tearing into each other. After that Cammy was living on borrowed time under Souness.

Graeme could be cruel, cutting people to ribbons when he needed to and not caring who got it, from Coisty to a cult hero like Scott Nisbet.

Once Nissy refused a move to Dundee, so the manager threw a Rothman's Football Yearbook at him and said: "Find yourself a club in there."

That one went into legend.

But he also stuck Scott in it again when we played down at Gretna in a match in aid of those bereaved by the Lockerbie bombing.

We had the Full Monty playing, all the stars apart from injured guys like myself and Coisty - though we felt we had to go for the trip anyway.

Despite our line-up we lost 3-2, yet Nissy still had that silly big grin on his face because he was an Edinburgh boy and had arranged a run home with the Gaffer.

Souness had settled in the capital in one of those understated houses of his - stables, a trout fishery, tennis court and swimming pool. Style.

Nissy was chirping: "Enjoy the bus ride, I'll be in the Merc."

Then he turned to Souness and said: "What time are we leaving at Gaffer?"

Graeme gave him that trademark steely glare and growled: "Nissy, I can't be ****ing bothered, get the ****ing bus."

A glum Nisbet trudged on to the coach with us and had to sprint to Queen Street to catch the last train home!

I had my run-ins with Graeme and in April 1988 he even kicked me out of the first team and accused me of being unprofessional. I was told there might be interest from Fiorentina at a time when he was fed up hearing tales of me being in trouble off the park.

Yet any confrontations I'd had with him paled into insignificance with one feud I had on the training pitch with one of the hardest men in British football. The frightening thing is, I started it! My wife Angela and my wee boy Max will tell you I'm moody at times, especially in the morning.

There are days when I wake up and I've fallen out with the world.

We were at war back then at times, me and the Gaffer. It was the one time I asked to leave Rangers and Souness called my bluff. I was furious about being forced to play out wide right when I wanted to be in the middle and I stormed into his office.

One thing led to another, I asked away and by the time I was trying to claw the words back into my stupid mouth he had said he'd arrange it.

So it was all simmering and I looked forward to the traditional Scotland-England match at training because he was always in the Sassenach side. I was going to give him the message.

Things are bumping at training and I come in and bowl him over before running away with my usual cheeky laugh. He was fuming and he floored me with a tackle which luckily I saw coming.

I rode the worst of it, bounced to my feet and grinned: "Is that your best shot?"

Even years on I shudder and wonder why the bloody hell I thought it was a good idea to say that to Souness.

He was gone by now, roaring about how he was going to punch my head off until the whole **SQUAD** tore in to break it all up.

My last image as I ran away is big Terry being pulled along as the Gaffer chased me. You know, I've heard Liverpool's Paul Ince say he's The Guv'nor - but I'd hate to have seen Souness in his prime.

The feud? Well, we did patch it up and I made it back in the side for the 2-2 draw with Celtic that ended up with Chris Woods, Terry Butcher and Frank McAvennie sent off.

Where did I play? Wide on the right!

I know my days at the club are numbered now, but I still love the debates with the Rangers fans about where the club has come from and where it's heading. The name of Souness is never far away.

Some will point out that previous managers never had the spending power he had, but the secret was he used it so well. He changed the whole face of our game and he took other clubs with him.

Teams like Celtic and Aberdeen had depended on their youth policy, but now all of a sudden that wasn't enough.

Anyway, a lot of managers get the money but Souness was one who bought the **RIGHT** people and it started with Terry Butcher.

We're talking about a man of presence again. He walked in and you knew you were looking at a giant of a footballer. Chris Woods and Graham Roberts were the same. Sure, they were English - but they had this incredible will to win. Men in the Souness mould.

It was typical of Graeme that when his Rangers reign kicked off on a boiling afternoon in Edinburgh it was MAYHEM. He got off to the worst possible start with that 2-1 defeat from Hibs at Easter Road in August 1986.

I've seen it all at Rangers but I have never known hype like there was before that match. It was at fever pitch. This was the biggest thing ever to hit Scottish football. *Rangers - Made in England* screamed the headlines.

Manchester United and Spurs had wanted Terry and Woods was their golden boy goalie. Yet we had them and even their arrogant papers paid a bit of attention to opening day.

They got their money's worth out of the trip north. In the first half there was a scuffle in the middle of the pitch between Souness and George McCluskey - and then all hell broke loose with the Gaffer sent off and me in the middle of it all.

At the time I didn't know what all the fuss was about. I missed Graeme lashing out and kicking McCluskey.

I was just in there, at the heart of this 21-man melee blindly swinging. I actually thumped one of my **OWN** players and got booked! Alan Rough was the only one who never made it into the book because it was too long a run for him to be bothered.

The dressing-room afterwards was silent, stunned. We'd been billed as invincible and we believed it.

Graeme had got caught up in the atmosphere, reacted to a couple of sly digs and elbows from Billy Kirkwood and it all fell about our ears.

Souness said nothing about it all afterwards. The lead was taken by the then-chairman David Holmes who came down to the dressing-room at Ibrox after Monday's training and told us to beware.

He told us this was a new era for the club and that we'd be hounded by the Press because of the bad start. He told us the spotlight was now well and truly on us. Twelve years later, it still is.

We beat Falkirk 1-0 in the midweek and in the next big home game against Dundee United we were two up thanks to Coisty. We felt we'd turned the corner.

But we blew it big-time in the second-half and lost 3-2. The Souness Revolution was off to a shocker.

Yet I knew he'd turn it round and I knew deep down that I would be a key part of it. I'd had a funny feeling he rated me before he arrived and before his first season even started I was offered a new four-year deal.

I signed on double lively, I still had a year of the current deal to go but they ripped that up. From 1984 to 1986 I had **TREBLED** my wages thanks to the esteem Souness held me in.

They advised me to keep sticking money in my pension scheme and I've done that to make my family's future secure. It was all so different from the way you do a contract now. These days my agent Blair Morgan advises me and goes through the fine print. Back then it was Souness and Walter Smith and I was too scared to say no!

Seriously, they wanted to build a team too and they never tried to short-change you. I was just 19 and Souness spoke to my mum and dad and the club said they'd look after me. They did then - and to the credit of men like the chairman David Murray they always have, despite seven operations on my knee since.

In that first season, though, there was no pain. Just gain.

We'd started to motor by the time I scored against Celtic in the first televised game on a Sunday from a dream pass from Davie Cooper. It was a reverse ball that took out a whole defence and how I missed moments like that when he left Rangers.

I would make, say, seven runs and Coop would lay on a plate for me four times. It was telepathy.

I have the same understanding with Ally and I'm sure he would tell you now that I still make the same runs during a game. Sure, I've lost a little pace because of the battering I've taken, but at 31 as I write this book I believe I can still do it.

Thing is. I'll now be doing it for someone other than Rangers.

But that was furthest from my mind three months into the Souness regime when we won Graeme his first trophy with a 2-1 win over Celtic in the Skol Cup Final.

What a match that was. Ref Davie Syme was hit on the head with a 50p piece and tried to red-card Tony Shepherd after he'd sent off Mo Johnston for trying to head-butt Stuart Munro.

I was just standing in the middle of the park thinking that Syme - the big medallion man - was only angry because the coin could have cut his face and ruined his suntan!

Derek Ferguson and I did really well in the middle of the park and I scored with my left foot from close-in before leaping the hoardings in front of the Rangers end.

Brian McClair kept them in it before we got a penalty late on when Roy Aitken fouled big Butcher. There was never any doubt in my mind that, despite all the tension, Coop would score.

I never saw him miss one and I always felt it was unfair on keepers that Davie was allowed to go one on one against them.

That spell was the best two seasons of Coop's life because Souness understood him. Graeme and Walter knew how to get the best of him. Davie came across as a huffy guy, but he was never the Moody Blue to me. He was a gem.

I used to pick him up for training in the morning, start babbling and he'd tell to shut up as he was doing his line for the bookie.

People said Souness came too late in his career but - God rest his soul - Davie always told me he wouldn't change a thing. I would have, though, in the aftermath of that Final as we hit the heights celebrating in front of the supporters.

There I was at 19 in dreamland then all these microphones were shoved in my face. It was my first time ever speaking on live TV and it was not one of the most memorable Durrant interviews.

I bumbled through the telly one and then I said on radio: "It was great. The ball from Cammy Fraser came down, hit me in the **BALLS** and I just blasted it in."

What can I say? I've learned a little since then, but the nerves got the better of me.

Europe in that first season with Souness was seen as a bonus not the be-all and end-all. How things have changed! We did well to get through against Finnish side Ilves Tampere and Portugal's Boavista before an unlucky exit against Borussia Monchengladbach.

I'd scored in the first leg, relishing Europe as always, but once more we lost a vital away goal and drew 1-1. I was injured for the return and we tied 0-0 this time to go out in a match when we had Davie Cooper and Stuart Munro sent off for *nothing* and were the victims of some scandalous refereeing decisions by a Belgian ref called Alexis Ponnet who was later involved in a bribes scandal.

We ended the first season of a revolution with two trophies. But we were to finish the second season falling apart at the seams and for me that's explained by one awful incident when Terry Butcher broke his leg.

His first season had been fantasy football but we were to struggle without him. I've always felt that was our **BEST** chance of winning the European Cup - yes, even better than when we were a goal away from the final in 1993.

We'd seen off Dynamo Kiev - when Graeme famously narrowed the pitch to set up a 2-0 win at Ibrox - and few who were there will forget the night of September 30, 1987.

It had been a battering over there at times, but we came back just a goal down and the Gaffer pulled his ploy to put the mockers on the likes of Vasily Rats and Oleg Blokhin out wide.

Alexei Mikhailitchenko played for Kiev, as did Oleg Kuznetsov, and when he later joined us he always insisted they had been duped and we were cheats!

We weren't, of course, we just had a manager who was a wide boy himself.

Souness played that night and he was superb when we were under fire and guarding a lead. Their keeper Viktor Chanov somehow threw the ball against Ally and Mark Falco scored before Coisty tied it up with one of his trademark efforts off the wrong corner of his head.

We held out and their keeper, who is probably still in the salt mines, ended up with a supporters' bus called the Viktor Chanov Loyal. For me that pitch-narrowing trick summed Souness up. Always thinking and never scared to takes things to the brink.

People slaughter his management skills but look at the side that beat a team who had won the Cup-Winners' Cup a year earlier. We've had more talented teams but it would take us five years to find one that blended together as well as this line-up:

Chris Woods, Jimmy Nicholl, Jimmy Phillips, John McGregor, Graeme Souness, Terry Butcher, Trevor Francis, Mark Falco, Ally McCoist, Yours Truly and Avi Cohen.

The likes of Francis - and later Ray Wilkins - brought some culture to Ibrox after their Italian travels but Jasper, so-called because he was the double of that comedian Jasper Carrott, was the victim of that season's best prank. I have to admit I had a hand in it.

We were in Dubai for the short-lived British Super Cup and we beat Everton on penalties to win this magnificent trophy. I've had the solid gold medal valued by the way - it nearly knocks you over when you pick it up and it's worth about £3,500. These Sultans do things in style.

Anyway, we were in the hotel and Trev's sitting nattering away to Ray in Italian and reading the Corriere dello Sport, a broadsheet paper that covers all the Serie A football.

He's hidden behind this big pink paper and I nicked up and set light to it, Francis was gibbering on for about a minute until he realised his Corriere was on fire and he leapt up screaming: "Bastards!"

I, of course, had fled the scene.

Back on the pitch, Gornik Zabrze were also dumped out of the European Cup but the quarter-final with Steaua Bucharest went against us after a torrid first 15 minutes over there in the first leg.

We came back trailing 2-0 and the media pundit Gerry McNee came back a very lucky man that he'd been separated from Souness after one of the game's most notorious bust-ups on the plane home.

I've had my run-ins with the Press in my time, but generally found most to be decent guys doing a job that's perhaps only bettered by playing. But there are times to talk to players and managers and times when most will know to leave well alone.

On the plane that day, McNee was fuming because an English paper had run a story on matchday that Coisty - who'd had a cartilage op just eight days before - would make a surprise return.

Their guy got his exclusive because he turned up at training the night before to watch and caught the fitness test. In the event Ally played well for 90 minutes and McNee was seething because he'd missed the story.

He started dishing out abuse to Graeme and like me the day Butcher and the rest held the Gaffer back I'm glad Souness never got at him. I never heard McNee - but I heard Graeme OK. Eyes bulging with anger he roared: "Don't you ever ****ing speak to me like that again."

He was pushed away, though, and never got to his target. Lucky man.

We were to win the second leg 2-1 but the damage was done and I've always felt that was a crying shame.

The signing deadline meant that we would have had Mark Walters, Ian Ferguson and John Brown in for the next round, three men who could have been the finishing touches.

PSV Eindhoven was the name on the trophy that year but with those players on board I firmly believe it would have been that of Rangers.

As for me? Souness had made things clear despite his disappointment at a season that never lived up to its billing.

He'd mapped out my future for me, told me how they would build the team around myself Derek and Ian Ferguson.

But one vicious tackle was to ruin everything.

CHAPTER 3

TO HELL AND BACK

PICK up a pencil and snap it. No effort. No time at all.

Now think how easily, how quickly, the career of the most gifted midfielder of a generation was wrecked.

In one split-second of venom at 3.08 on October 8, 1988, Ian Durrant took a set of studs on his right knee and his ligaments snapped.

Simple as blinking. One moment he is planning his next sliderule pass, the next he is a hair's breadth from being finished

Seven operations. More than 1000 stitches. A bitter court battle. Months of rehabilitation. Years of thinking what might have been.

All caused by a single kick in the blink of an eye.

Ian Durrant's is the classic tale of how perilous the life of a footballer can be.

And this is the story of the aftermath of the moment that did for him, a tale of twisted minds and bitter hatred which caused Durrant almost as much pain as Neil Simpson's boot had.

I STOOD and stared at the letter I'd opened up in the Ibrox foyer.

It was an envelope full of poison.

For a few seconds I couldn't quite take in the photograph it contained. My mind wouldn't let me believe someone could send me something so sick, so twisted.

Then shock was replaced by anger, boiling anger at the scumbags who could take out the bitterness they felt for me on the most helpless soul in the world.

As I stood there, gaze locked on that photograph like a rabbit caught in headlights, I knew the pain I'd suffered in Aberdeen on the worst day of my career would never be over.

The picture I was looking at had been taken only a few days earlier, on one of the happiest occasions of my life. It was of me in hospital with Angela and our new-born baby son Max.

Anyone who has seen their child born will know how I felt that day two and a bit years ago - but if I was high then, you will never know how low I got when I opened up that envelope to find a photocopy of those smiling scenes doctored to give a sick twist.

So-called Aberdeen fans had drawn bandages on Max's knee with the chilling message that said: *"Hope you end up like your dad"*.

I looked at the scrawled words for a signature, some kind of sign-off, but of course there was none. No one who could do such a thing would have the guts to sign a name.

And as I read the note over and over I wondered what kind of mind could think up a cruel stunt like that. It's hard for me to understand, hard to believe someone can hate me that much.

It's hard to talk about too - just how do you make sense of something like that? But I'm open with my wife about things like that and I showed her it. I knew she'd be upset, but she'd have been worse if I'd hidden it from her and she had found out later.

So we talked it through together, but I realised that I will never work it out. The Dons fans seem to think I am to blame for something in the whole sorry Neil Simpson controversy.

And ever since October 8, 1988 they have made life hell for me.

I get obscene letters and they sing some song about me lying on the ground with my leg snapped in two. Every time I go to Pittodrie I am made a scapegoat yet I was the **VICTIM**.

I get sick hatemail all the time saying it was justice, that I got what I deserved. I even have some stuff in the house from a guy who writes to me almost every time I even go up there to play their **RESERVES**.

The last time I played there he insisted, wrongly, that I ran off without shaking Toni Kombouare's hand and wrote: "Always remember that you got what you deserved. I wouldn't piss on you if you were on fire."

That sort of thing shocks other people to the core, but me? I'm used to it now - after all, they've been piling it on to me for a decade.

But that letter about Max? Well, that *did* shock and sicken me, right down to the pit of my stomach. Not content with the injury I got, the huge chunk of my career it took away or all the grief I went through they're now wishing ill on my son.

Just when you think these people have sunk as low as they can go they go lower to new depths. I even have relatives in Canada who tell me Aberdeen fans over there have me as their Public Enemy No.1 and they probably haven't ever seen the Dons play.

It's ingrained in these people now, part of their culture to excuse their player and blame me. It's bizarre - blame me for *what*?

Those letters started right after the game and within weeks they had T-shirts printed giving me stick. At first it wound me up so much that I was physically scared of playing up there again.

I try to take it with a pinch of salt these days, remind myself I am not dealing with normal people here, but with **MORONS**.

Those letters were only worth using as toilet paper, but they're hi-tech now and they even abuse me on the Internet. Some Aberdeen fans' page is filled with the same poison.

When we sat down to write this book I knew, of course, that one heartbreaking day in 1988 would be at the core of it all.

They say time is a healer, but after a decade it hasn't healed my pain because the memories still hurt as much as the physical scars I carry to this day.

There's one thing people forget about that day. There had been been skirmishes to set a tone and there was an ugly atmosphere - fuelled for the Aberdeen fans by the sight of their old player Neale Cooper in a Rangers jersey for the first time.

Think about it, when I went down we were only eight minutes into the game and already we were at fever pitch.

Things don't usually get so heated so quickly but they did this time and although Neil Simpson had been involved in a couple of dust-ups I looked up and relaxed when ref Louis Thow blew his whistle for a foul.

Vision. The one thing every critic said I had on a pitch then, the ability to see things other players couldn't.

Sometimes you will glance and see things out of the corner of your eye in an instant but I simply didn't see Simpson coming.

I eased up and pulled out of the tackle thinking the action would stop, looking to tame the ball and maybe take a quick free-kick. Souness has since said I was naive and maybe's he's right. It was a costly mistake.

The next second, **BANG**! I was on the ground and I never knew anything about it. To this day I have never been able to bring myself to watch it on television. All I know about what went on around me is what I have read or been told by those who were there.

I crumpled to the turf and within a split-second the pain was pulsing through me. I knew something major had gone wrong in my knee.

It blew up straight away and with every little bit of swelling came more misery and hurt. I knew I was in big trouble.

At Pittodrie the fans are so close to the pitch you can hear every boo or shout. But everything was blanked from my mind - it was like TV white noise in my head. Nothing else seemed to exist in the whole world but the torrent of messages coming from my knee. As I lay there, before some late-coming fans were even settled in their seats, I was only aware of one sensation.

PAIN.

It was an injury that would spark many theories. I heard all the stuff about how the physio Phil Boersma carrying me off is supposed to have wrecked my knee but that's honestly wide of the mark.

I was on the ground for what seemed like an eternity and I could feel movement all over the place inside my knee. I begged and pleaded to get off but still no stretcher came.

I was in **AGONY** by now and I just wanted to get off there. I started getting naughty with Phil, screaming at him: "You bastard, get me off this ****ing pitch."

He was shaken. He took a rush of blood to the head and carried me off, but every doctor I have spoken to since has assured me the damage was already done.

The hurt of that blow to my knee is without question the worst pain I have ever experienced.

If I tell you that I was given **TWO** injections in the dressing-room by our club doctor Donald Cruickshank simply to dull the pain a little - *dull* it, mind you, not *kill* it - then it will give you some idea.

Little gestures in the times of your deepest need tell you a lot about people. And I'll never forget that David Holmes sat with me through the whole game and tried to calm me.

He told me: "I won't allow anything bad to happen to you. Whatever the damage this club will pay the money to fix it.

"We'll stand by you, Ian, I promise you that."

I remember being so distressed by his words because I thought I was looking at six or eight weeks out with ligament damage. Six or eight weeks? Offer me that now and I'd give you three years wages in return.

That was a venomous match at Pittodrie and I felt even worse when we eventually lost 2-1. Big Terry went ballistic at the end and kicked in the dressing-room door but I was sedated by then and I couldn't really take in the full extent of what had happened. I heard the word "cruciate"

40

but I was out of it and I didn't really know what it meant anyway. Within a matter of months I'd be an expert.

I was stretchered out of Pittodrie still clad in my kit and the Dons fans were even screaming abuse at me on the way to the bus.

The journey home was one of constant pain - it was becoming a blur by now because I was heavily sedated and I was strapped in to make sure I didn't move the knee, jar it and do even more damage.

Four hours after I'd been taking possession and sizing up my next pass I was in Ross Hall Hospital in Glasgow getting a bed bath. By then the knee was massive, puffed up like a balloon.

Surgeon Peter Scott assessed the damage and when he ordered me not to eat anything I knew right away I was getting an anaesthetic and going for an orthoscope the next day.

Meanwhile, my pal Derek Ferguson - out of favour with Souness at the time - was in a city centre pub waiting on me.

He hadn't travelled up but had listened to the match on radio. They'd said I was injured, but Del expected me to be strapped up and out that night. He sat on in the pub with a friend. They would have a long wait.

I was dazed when I woke up from that first four-hour op and looked through haze to the end of the bed where the surgeon, Doc Cruickshank, the gaffer, Walter Smith and the chairman all waited.

That was when I knew that it was something bad and then Mr Scott said six words that left me reeling. He looked up sternly and warned: "You may **NEVER** play football again."

I had ruptured three ligaments and badly stretched another and when they all trooped out of the room like mourners after a funeral the tears welled up in my eyes.

I was 21 and they were as good as saying it was over. I was determined almost immediately to prove that I was young enough to come back.

Yet I knew from the gut reaction of Souness and Smith, the grim look on their faces, that they felt one of their better players had been taken away from them.

They were shocked by the extent of the injury yet they were to leave no stone unturned to get me fit again no matter what it cost. Rangers were as good as the chairman's word.

But these were dark times for me. I went back to stay with my parents and there were still times when I was in agony with the knee.

At the time I was talking about buying the District Bar and it might have been a good move because they were getting plenty of my cash over the bar anyway.

I had a few Saturday sessions on the sauce after which I'd sleep on the fold-down bed in my mum's living-room and wake up with a mighty hangover feeling sorry for myself. It was a bad time for me. No way am

41

I hiding that. One minute I'd had everything and now I felt I had nothing. I'm not the first player to have a bevvy when they are low and I won't be the last. But I came through.

I had no trade and the one thing I could do properly had been taken away in a flash but always inside there was the desire to play again.

There are times when the only word to describe how you feel is alone. I still went to the games because I was a Rangers fan before I was a Rangers player - but you feel as if the last thing players need is someone hobbling around feeling sorry for himself.

I had to find a way back and I finally found it because I became a pioneer. You don't get many of those from Kinning Park.

Peter Scott did a great job on my knee and I got another huge boost when I was at Ross Hall and Craig Levein of Hearts came to visit me.

Craig had been through the same thing and he was more like a doctor than a player. He knew everything and he talked me through it all. He told me that I was facing a mental battle as well as a physical one and by God he was right.

With all that help it took me just 18 months to believe that I was back.

I made it into the reserves and landed my first comeback on February 10, 1990 - 18 months after the injury - and felt I'd made it. My first touch was a header that went adrift, but I didn't care because 5,085 punters turned out to see me past any setbacks like that in a Reserve League Cup tie against Hearts.

I was touched before that match when John McGregor came up in the dressing-room and handed me the skipper's armband. It was the first time I'd ever captained the club and leading the side out was an honour.

What a game to come back in, too. We battered through 120 goalless minutes and then went to penalties. I scored mine but we lost out 7-6.

Then I played against Dunfermline reserves in midweek and the fans turned out to back me as they always have with another crowd of 4,000 as we beat the Pars 1-0.

I even got on the scoresheet with a late penalty after Davie Dodds had been pushed in the box - and dared to hope I really was back.

But underneath it all I was kidding myself, because there wasn't enough movement in the knee to sustain a career in the Premier League.

I always remember the Doc saying my knee was more like something you should see after a road smash and not a football match. The damage had been so bad that the knee just wasn't strong enough.

Yet I was buzzing and Souness told me I was looking like my old self again. I was even on the verge of the first team again when all of a sudden - **SNAP!** A ligament went again in training.

Here I was, back to square one and I have to admit that this time I thought I was finished. But still the Doc, Smith and Souness took me into the treatment room and told me there was an op in America I could try that involved using a dead man's tendon to strengthen my knee.

I didn't want to know at first because by now I had hit so many walls and I simply didn't feel I could keep going.

But in April, I decided to go for it and I was off to the Sherman Oakes Community Hospital in California where they specialised in rescuing the careers of American football players and basketball stars.

There I gritted my teeth and the magic of Dr Dominic Blazina saved my career. By the time I came back the following year I'd had seven operations, ground-breaking surgery to put the dead man's tendon in my knee and I'd cost the club around £40,000 in doctor's bills.

That was the doctor's bills for rebuilding my knee. No amount of cash could settle the bill for those who rebuilt my spirit.

That first debt is owed to Rangers Football Club, the second to Doc Cruickshank. I've always been a man for jokes and wind-ups and even in those depressing times you really had to laugh - especially when your travelling companion was the Doc.

You can't fly for two weeks after the op and I faced a nervous time recuperating in San Francisco. The Doc's prescription this time was to take me out to some of his favourite restaurants to down some clam chowder and red wine. Sadly because of my crutches I couldn't get across to Alcatraz for the tour but we did the next best thing.

There I was in a restaurant called the Neptune's Palace, looking over to the famous prison where they'd film *The Rock* eating lobster and thinking life wasn't too bad after all.

Trouble was the Doc paid with the club American Express and lifted **BOTH** copies of the receipt leaving no record we'd settled the bill.

I went to hobble on to the car on my crutches and he came out to catch up but I could sense something had gone wrong. There were guys with walkie-talkies following us and I was starting to think there must be a burglary going on somewhere.

Then they swooped on **US** because they thought we hadn't paid! There I was just out of hospital - and close to arrest from four gun-toting cops. I'd love to see what the papers would have done with *that* story if it had got out back home!

Next up, the car hire nightmare. We get in this motor, drive off and I say to him: "Doc, when did you buy that fruit?"

He says: "What fruit? I didn't buy any fruit. Jesus Christ, Durranty...this isn't our car!"

So we quickly had to dump that one at the roadside and go back for the real one before we got rumbled again.

What a man the Doc is. I've always felt these things only happen to him because his brain is going so much quicker than everyone else's.

He'll always have a special place in my heart.

San Francisco, America to Lilleshall, England. Bit of a difference and for the second time since the Simpson tackle I was in rehab.

I knew when I went down there for a second nine-month stint under Grant Downie - now the physio at Ibrox - that it would be testing. I owe Grant a lot, because he was the one who pushed me when I was beginning to feel really low about myself.

I had to get away then, away from Glasgow, away from everything around me and away from Ibrox. It was starting to do my nut in. I didn't mind watching the games but coming in every day was constantly reminding me of what I was missing and I couldn't take it any more.

Lilleshall helped - but there are bad memories too, thoughts that linger of being away from home when my dad died and not being able to play the game I love.

Grant was like family to me but once more no-one helped more than my mum. I wasn't some kind of monster constantly on benders who could drink George Best under the table.

The truth is that I felt sorry for myself, sorry for what had happened to me. I'm not the first person to drink to forget problems.

I buckled down when my dad died in August 1989 and helped my mum through it just as she helped me through my injury problems.

The boys in Ibrox called me Oliver Reed, just the type of humour that keeps you smiling through the bad times. Despite the sweat and the tears at Lilleshall I also remember the place and smile.

I met some characters, from Norman Whiteside and Alan Hansen in football to Ian Woosnam in golf and jockey Peter Scudamore. Each had one aim - to get fit so they never had to see each other again!

We used to play volleyball at the end of the day but the catch was that you had to sit down. Believe me, these games were as fiercely contested as the FA Cup Final, the Open or the Grand National because if you lost the penalty was a five-mile ride on the mountain bikes.

So here were all these top sportsmen going daft over this stupid game because they knew they'd get extra exercises if they lost.

I'm screaming "Lettuce Wrists!" at these jockeys because they were always useless. At the end of a fortnight when Woosie was there with his bad back he had to return to the golf course to test his fitness.

There was an enormous scrap to get on that foursome - needless to say I blew it. When Scu was there the banter also flowed, but I still couldn't **BUY** a tip off the man.

By now Grant was bike-mad and he had this run that actually took you through three counties on the 12-mile route.

We were fed-up with it all and I had the injured Ally McCoist - down recovering from a badly torn hamstring - and Whiteside for company.

A dangerous mix.

Ally's spirits needed lifting because he had gone to a specialist called Richard Smith in Holland and even he couldn't cure it.

What can I say? We took a shortcut and sat for 45 minutes at a country inn having coffee and doughnuts and spinning the bikes' pedals to get the numbers up before returning to base in great nick!

That's when you discover your friends. When you can pick each other up when you're on a downer. That's what rehab is all about for a player.

I'd be in there and some other guy would limp in worse off than me to start out on the road back. You'd talk to each other, cajole each other and get each other through it.

It was a great set-up there, often training with 25 footballers and then going on a bike run 12-handed. No lonely times to feel sorry for yourself again. And I was away from Glasgow where half the city would throw bottles at me if I went on a bike run!

Yep, the laughs kept me going but always the shadow was there over my career. What would I do if I never made it back?

That's why I went to the law for compensation, I felt I had to do it because of what was taken away from me.

Nowadays I'm grown up enough to know that while I've suffered Neil has suffered too. The case was hard for both of us and we at last settled out of court in 1993.

Afterwards, he described the settlement as a "weight off my mind and my family's." He said it had dragged on for four years and it had been a "rotten time."

Well, it wasn't much fun for me either and from what had been a £2million damages claim I walked out with about £330,000.

That and the legal costs of £500,000 were paid out from a Scottish League insurance fund that all the clubs pay into.

There were plans to call Coisty as my star witness because he, more than perhaps anyone, knew what I had lost financially and the pain I had gone through.

In the end I just wanted it sorted. I was happy with the settlement because I could have waited years for a verdict. But I wanted something done and that meant the law.

Certainly, the SFA had done nothing. I lost two-and-a-half years and Simpson was given a yellow card - that doesn't tally up.

I had to make a stand, not just for myself but for future players who could be put through the same ordeal as I was.

OK, I got money. But I lost international caps, a World Cup place, a European Championships, appearance money, win bonuses and a huge slice of my career. Cash was a poor substitute.

I was a mainstay of the Scotland team back in 1988, but I missed out at

Italia '90 and that hurt so much because my dad had planned to go with two of his pals and was making all the arrangements before he died.

He was convinced I'd be back for Scotland by then, but it wasn't to be.

I went to the Finals in any case and had a few drinks on a great night out watching us beat Sweden 2-1 in Genoa, but it just wasn't the same.

There was this lump of grief inside me, an ache because I knew I should have been playing on the biggest stage of all instead of sitting with the Tartan Army. Looking back, I'm sure I'd have been in the game's Hall of Fame with over 50 caps by the time I was 25.

Instead, what do I have to look back on? Eleven caps and what might have been. I was to get back to a peak in 1992-93 but I'd lost pace - after seven ops you're not going to be Linford Christie any more.

Yet I still have my awareness and my passing ability and although I haven't played as much as I'd have liked in the last few years maybe Walter has protected me too much.

Who knows? Whatever the truth I simply find it hard to say anything against the man because he has always looked after me.

He knows and I know that on that fateful day back in 1988 I was 21 and I was at my peak. I was valued at £3m a decade ago and I felt I could have gone on to play anywhere.

I feel I could have lived up to Graeme's prediction and played in Italy but I never got the chance.

If any kid was offered a big opportunity like that now I'd tell him to go for it in a minute. You're never too young because you can always learn when you're there.

As for learning, the day my career hung in the balance was to teach me many lessons about life as well as football.

There were a few times when I thought I would never get back but that's when you're thankful for having people like my missus around.

Angela has been great for me despite the fact that it all started in 1987 when I fell over a hedge in Benidorm and she was lying there.

She's a lovely blonde and I thought she was Swedish - only to be slightly disappointed when I found out she was from Dennistoun! But we've got through it all just the same.

Angela and the family mean so much to me. The lowest point may have been my dad's death and the injury, but the high points have to be getting married and the birth of the kids.

As for Neil Simpson? I have never said one word to him since the day he decked me. Even the court case was carried out between lawyers.

When he was at Newcastle United I remember he told a paper it was good news for football that I was back but he has never apologised or tried to contact me to explain what he did.

But who knows how I would have taken that anyway?

46

Am I bitter? Yes, of course I am. Only a saint would not be. But I can't dwell on it or I'd start losing myself in remorse over it again. I've come through it, I won't let it ruin my life.

I still say to young kids at Rangers now that they couldn't lace my boots when I was their age. Yet it's just a hollow joke because the truth is I'll never know how high I could have gone.

The other thing that hurts a lot still is that my dad didn't see me make my comeback, but I have to move on.

Neil Simpson is coaching kids up north and has got on with his life as best he could. I can't argue with him looking at it that way, because the same goes for me.

But, yes, there are still times when it hits home. It might be when I'm getting painful manipulation on the knee, or something completely unconnected - but suddenly the incident is in my mind.

I sit there at these moments and I'm not ashamed to say I curse the name Neil Simpson. Even now.

To be honest I don't think I will **EVER** speak to Simpson again. Our paths are unlikely to cross professionally and, let's face it, we're hardly likely to go looking for each other.

You know, people say to me: "If the tables had been turned would you have phoned him at hospital to apologise and see how he was?"

I reply: "Stupid question...because I would NEVER have tackled a fellow player like that."

The picture of the tackle, that famous grainy shot, is in this book. Take a good, close look at the expression on Simpson's face. He went in to snap me in two and I could never do that.

So am I bitter? Yes, I am.

Ten years later, ten years after an opponent went into a tackle on a football pitch with hurt on his mind, I still have a sour taste in my mouth.

Some scars will never heal.

CHAPTER 4

THE COMEBACK - ONE GOAL FROM GLORY

THIRTY months of anguish ended with a first-team comeback on the dramatic title run-in of 1991 and now Durrant and Rangers were on the threshold of greatness once more.

The slower pace, the emphasis on passing skills, the need for clever runs and the class to glean a goal. Ian Durrant was MADE for the European football stage.

That was never more evident than in season 1992-93 when he was the inspiration behind a glory run that took Treble-winning Gers to within an ace of the Champions' Cup Final.

This is the story of a Rangers team that peaked together, from Goram to Gough through McCall and McCoist.

It's the tale of the team Durrant firmly believes was the greatest in the club's HISTORY.

THE seeds of my best season in a Rangers jersey were sown on a chilly afternoon in February 1991 in what was meant to be a low-key comeback from my knee injury in the reserves against Hibs.

All you dream about when you are on the comeback trail is playing again - then the games come around and you almost freeze with the apprehension. At the time of the comeback I had a flat in Bothwell, but I stayed with my mum before that game.

I couldn't settle that night and I was up at the crack of dawn for a bowl of cereal, to read the papers about the first team's game at Motherwell, anything to try and occupy myself.

But I just couldn't settle and for a player not normally afflicted by the jitters I was in new territory. I was a bag of nerves and I was in at Ibrox at 11 in the morning.

I stuck some kit on and wandered around, this was it. This was when it mattered for me. I knew my career was on the line.

My body-clock was AWOL that day and I was first in to the Players' Lounge for lunch.

I wandered up the marble staircase and turned left into our little haven still remembering the Souness advice and ploughing into a bowl of pasta to stock up on my carbohydrates. After 28 months out of the game I knew I was going to need the energy to survive a match.

Eventually we were in the dressing-room and I headed straight for my peg to haul on my favourite jersey, the No.10. I'd asked especially that I could wear it on my return because I feel it holds luck for me.

I only ever lost it at Ibrox through injury and a guy called Mark Hateley claimed it. I never chinned him for two good reasons:

(A) *He was bigger than me,*

(B) *He was superb.*

Every time he was injured, though, it was back where it belonged...on my back! I was glad I had my talisman on that day because the doubts were still swimming around in my head about the injury.

I wore a bandage over my right knee when I ran out. I still don't know why. I didn't need it but I was scarred on the outside and maybe I was scarred inside too.

It was still preying on my mind, I know that much.

The emotions of a footballer are easily laughed at and I'll admit to anyone that this is a nasty and cynical game at times.

But I'm telling you the truth when I say that when I emerged from the tunnel and there were 5,000 chanting my name I was deeply touched.

Can you imagine what I felt like when 15 minutes into the match the crowd had risen to 16,000? My bottle crashed! The club just hadn't anticipated a response like that and I was stunned too.

They hadn't opened enough turnstiles and they were leading fans down the track while the game was going on to get them seats. I just couldn't believe it and to this day I can't.

There I was in the middle of it all and the chants of "He's blue, he's white, he's ****ing dynamite! Ian Durrant, Ian Durrant" were ringing round me once more.

Those songs mean so much to you as a player, to be special and have your own chant. It's what you dream of as a kid.

I'm sure Coisty or Lauders still feel a little humble when they hear *Super Ally* or *Walking in a Laudrup Wonderland* and I know the last time I hear my own song will bring the tears flooding. It's hard to sum up what it meant after all I'd been through to hear that again on my comeback.

And it also gave me a physical lift because even that early I felt the pace. Those people turning up to support me gave me more adrenalin and the incentive not to chuck it.

I settled in and got through the 90 minutes but my eventual comeback owes a debt to every one of the people who turned up that day. I still look back and think it must have been a dream.

I'd made a short-lived attempt before that against Dunfermline and broke down but that day I felt I was back and I've never had any serious fitness problems since.

The first team comeback came against Hibs on April 6, 1991 in a 0-0 draw and despite the result and Andy Goram's stormer for the Hibees - a performance which I'm sure helped him earn a move to Ibrox - I was so pleased with myself.

There had been an incredible build-up to that match with the Ticket Office inundated and opened up specially on the Saturday morning to accommodate a sell-out, it was like a cup final. My Cup Final.

I'd been out for all that time, it had been such a hard road and I remember the feeling of joy I had simply because I had lasted 90 minutes in a Rangers' top team again.

It was the day I knew I could cope because Callum Milne had a couple of pops at me. I didn't expect favours but the knee stood up to it and that was so important.

The following week against St Johnstone I scored with a left foot curler into the corner as we won 3-0, although I'm still convinced to this day that my old Ibrox pal Lindsay Hamilton felt sorry for me and let it in!

Seriously, that was a day that showed that although I might be back, the match-fitness was missing because Brian Reid got sent off and the strain of playing for a ten-man team floored me.

After 70 minutes I hit the brick wall. I knew I wasn't right and it was out of the limelight and back to the quiet of the reserves for a fortnight.

It was after that match that we heard the bombshell news. Graeme Souness was defecting to Liverpool just when we had that title run-in to cope with. I was shellshocked by his decision because I had a great rapport with him, but he had a burning desire to go back to Anfield. He couldn't help himself but take the job.

Yet for me it was a mistake to go there and even Graeme might admit that now. It broke a lot of hearts in the stands and it broke mine. But the stick he got was a shame. He never deserved that.

Rangers were light years behind what they should have been until Souness arrived and dragged us up to date.

As we came to terms with his departure and Walter's appointment we had a league to win and I was in the stiffs again.

But I scored a hat-trick at Hamilton Accies to help us win the Reserve League West and all of a sudden I was in the frame for a place in Scottish football's biggest game since Hearts faced Killie who won the title on the last day of the season in 1965.

For the first time in 26 years, two teams in with a chance of winning the league would go head-to-head on the last day of the season.

And after all I'd gone through since that nightmare afternoon three years before who did we face? Aberdeen.

Walter Smith was calm that day in the dressing-room but he must have known if the Dons reached their height we were in trouble because we were down to the bare bones by then.

I will always be eternally grateful to the Gaffer for giving me a chance and I feel it was a day that summed up the true Rangers. If you want to talk about people playing for the jersey watch the video of that day.

There are Aberdeen players who must still regret that match because a few of them didn't fancy it. They may never have another opportunity like it. Peter van de Ven and Hans Gillhaus missed key chances - and they paid for it when Mark Hateley hit them with a classic one-two.

He had rattled through their young keeper Michael Watt early doors and that unsettled the boy from then on.

Mind you, even a guy on the top of his form would have been helpless by our opening goal. As Mark Walters shaped to cross, Mark ran Alex McLeish inside out and timed his jump perfectly to bullet in a classic.

The second came after a scuffed shot by Mo Johnston - but there's no doubt Watt could have held it had he not had one eye on the charging Hateley. Instead, he palmed the ball out and the big fella rattled in the rebound.

From then on we were always going to win it and we deserved to because we came through even though we were the walking wounded.

Big Mark ended up at **LEFT-BACK** and I played wide left, wide right and then just in behind the strikers. Full-back Tom Cowan played on with a broken leg and John Brown's Achilles snapped - by the end we were all just hoofing the ball anywhere. But we did it.

51

By the end of the following season, after conquering more niggles and knocks and a lengthy spell in the reserves, I was edging towards the real Ian Durrant again.

Scotland boss Andy Roxburgh still shocked me, though, when he said he wanted me to go Canada with the squad on the warm-up tour before the European Championship Finals in Sweden. I would loved to have gone and I will look back in years to come and think I should have.

But I spoke to the Gaffer - who'd given me a new three-year deal in the March of that year after I'd been linked with a move to Dundee - and he has never done me a bad turn. He looked me right in the eye and said: "Durranty, you're not fit enough yet, you won't do yourself justice."

In the end it was **MY** decision and after a fortnight's to-ing and froing I decided against it.

I knew I wasn't 100 per cent because I was spending every afternoon in bed resting from the strain of keeping myself on track and I'd played 54 first team and reserve games in a crunch season for my career.

So instead of travelling the world with my country, I went on a long summer break, came back flying and went on to have my best ever season for Rangers.

But, yes, it was a very hard shout turning down a chance like that.

Scotland never let themselves down at the finals - they still never have during my career - and it would have been nice to be a part of it.

My own European run was just around the corner, though.

It all started against Danish side Lyngby at Ibrox and, aside from the tension, my abiding memory is the brilliant display of a loping, gangling midfielder called Morten Wieghorst. He was really impressive as we edged a 2-0 win through Mark Hateley and Pieter Huistra and I'd soon know all about big Morten at Dundee and then Celtic.

I remember Hateley took a boot in the face to score his header that night, typical bravery of a player who - behind McCoist - is the best striker I've played with at Ibrox.

I respected him not only for his football but for the inner strength he showed. He had an awful start at Ibrox after coming to the club injured but he left a hero.

He was Billy Big Time at first, turning up to training in a Ferrari with a £10,000 suit while I was still shopping at What Everyone Wants!

He was a good laugh, though, and I can exclusively deny those stories that he scrapped with Duncan Ferguson for cutting the lapels off one of his famous Versace jackets. I was friendly with Dunc right from the off because we changed next to each other.

I had been No.10 but the kitman Jimmy Bell moved me when I got injured because he said that number was unlucky now. I was switched to No.12 and Duncan had No.14, right underneath the picture of the

Queen in our dressing-room. Pub rumours about feuds between Mark and Dunc got out of hand but the truth is they **DID** have one memorable boxing match.

We were at our training camp at Il Ciocco in Tuscany and after three weeks of hard work the leash was off and we went out for a few bevvies.

A fight kicked off at the back of the bus and when I looked back there was Hateley and Ferguson going at it - they were split up but I wasn't going anywhere near.

I would have backed Hateley, by the way, he had more time in the ring behind him!

But there was no question of those two being sworn enemies. Mark saw Duncan as a threat to his jersey and that was it. He reacted to the threat by scoring goals for fun.

Those bus scraps would start with people throwing things at each other and then it would be a free-for-all. If you had a ring on someone might get marked but you learned to time your digs in the ribs.

That was certainly Walter's ploy when Graeme Souness sent him up the back to sort one brawl out - and he was an expert!

Those bouts were always the end of a night letting off steam after a few beers, but it was never the sign of people hating each other. Who could question our team spirit?

Bevvy and Rangers; a gossip columnist's dream that has maybe been fuelled by the skipper Richard Gough saying that the team that drinks together, wins together.

Now if we were smashed as many times as we're supposed to have been we'd have been too blitzed to pick up the trophies - but there is truth in what Goughie says.

We used those times together to sort out any backbiting or problems that there were and emerged as a **TEAM**. And for me that '93 side had the best spirit of any team I have known at Ibrox.

We needed it in that second leg in Copenhagen's magnificent Parken Stadium and once again the punters stick in my mind.

It was a stunning arena, one of the best I've ever had the pleasure of playing in and Walter Smith's blue and white army stormed it.

We had over 5,000 there with us and it was a great night that peaked when we broke away and I skipped round the keeper to roll the ball home for the only goal. *Magic.*

Who would we get in the next round? It looked like Stuttgart when they beat Leeds - but the Germans had played four foreigners instead of the permitted three and after that reprieve Howard Wilkinson's side won a play-off in Barcelona.

They champions of England had held up their end of the bargain ...and the Battle of Britain was on!

That game will go down in legend. The dressing-room beforehand was a scene of complete determination to do the job.

And in the midst of it all was John Brown, diehard bluenose.

The hype had been astonishing beforehand but Bomber had gone beyond hype. He was a man **POSSESSED**.

John is a calm figure...until ten minutes before kick off when he turns into Hannibal Lecter's mad brother. He's slapping you on the back to encourage you, but it's bloody **SORE**.

He's physically hurting you, but you'd never dare tell him because you're just happy he is on your side.

So he's going bonkers and the Gaffer and Archie are striding round shouting: "Bomber, remember, stick to Cantona. Durranty, don't let McAllister dictate it."

But in all honesty they didn't really have to do anything to motivate us. We had been fired up enough by the posing posse of arrogant English journalists who'd been telling us we were going to fall flat on our faces.

As I stood in the tunnel at two minutes to kick-off, I vowed to savour every moment of this one. I looked across at the faces of experienced campaigners like Gary McAllister and Gordon Strachan and they told a fascinating story.

They knew they had no real support behind them, very unusual for Leeds wherever they play, and their nerves were there for all to see.

But if we thought they weren't up for it, we were wrong.

Gary must have calmed down quickly enough - because within a minute he'd taken a half-clearance from a corner and banged a stunning volley into the top corner. There was utter silence around the stadium, except for the muted cheering of a handful of Leeds punters who had beaten the official ban on travelling fans.

They couldn't help but leap out of their seats when Gary's shot boomed past Andy Goram - one of them was Strach's dad, who managed to get himself thrown out for celebrating.

The patter flew on the park that night - and as we regrouped, Gary ran past Coisty grinning: "What about that wee strike!"

Then I swerved in a corner, their keeper John Lukic couldn't cope with my trademark spin and he punched it into his own net - yet I didn't get the credit! Amazing!

Now we were flying and Coisty picked up the scraps when Dave McPherson's header was saved. Two-one. Now Ibrox was bouncing and so were we - I laughed like a drain when Coisty sprinted past Macca and screamed: "What about **THAT** wee strike, eh?"

That night taught me a lot about self-preservation as a pro and all the lessons came from Gordon Strachan, whose jersey I swapped at the end.

At the time all the publicity was about his porridge and banana diet and I remember thinking I should go on that if he was playing like that at the age of 35. An incredible player.

When the dust settled, we went to Elland Road 2-1 up...but still the arrogance was there from the English. I did a Press conference and from the questions I was being asked you could tell deep down that they still felt it was a case of how many we'd be thumped by.

Their journalists were so cocky and John Sadler in The Sun summed their attitude up with a piece in that vein.

It said infuriating things like: *"You can write off Rangers, they had their chance at Ibrox."*

Did we need any more incentive to win than that?

Stuart McCall, who'd grown up a Leeds fan, was raging and cut the piece out to stick on the dressing room wall - every shred of the guy's arrogance was stored away and used as motivation.

That wasn't the first stuff to go up there. You always have someone who wants to be smart and take a pop at Rangers and that's where their handiwork ends up. We use it to gee ourselves.

So the Rangers side which arrived at Elland Road for the return leg was fired up, don't you worry. Even when they tried to psyche us by blasting out Eye of the Tiger as we came onto the pitch we stayed 110 per cent focused.

I stood in the tunnel in those last few seconds before the off, shadow-boxing and winding up any Leeds player who came near me!

There's this feeling on nights like that, just before you go out into the roar. You're going into a lion's den and the hairs stand on end on the back of your neck. I love it. I had a further spur, a feeling that they were all against us and the knowledge that we could sicken them.

And I knew in my heart that the Rangers fans would get in somehow, they always do. For a start, my brothers and a mate made it after some naughty player gave them tickets!

They saw me win a header - and there's a rarity - to set up big Hateley for an incredible volley that gave us the early lead and rammed all those English words back down their throats.

Ally then swooped in at the far post to score a classic diving header and although we lost a late one to Cantona we'd done it - we were kings of Britain and in the Champions League.

What a night. We stayed down in Leeds and celebrated in style.

I'll never forget a slightly rumpled, worse-for-wear Gaffer coming down to the hotel foyer at 7am to see Stuart McCall and I downing champers and raising a glass to him. He muttered: "Do you think we should perhaps stop drinking? We do have a match on Saturday..."

We did too - and it was against Celtic! But still we pulled it off again as I scored in a 1-0 win at their place. What a week!

That Champions League adventure was to start against Marseille at Ibrox and it was bewildering that we got a 2-2 draw because, putting it quite simply, we had been **MURDERED**.

People often say to me that was the best Rangers comeback ever - but I simply look upon that game as a team dropping their guard. For 70 minutes we were taught a footballing lesson.

To his eternal credit the manager brought on Gary McSwegan, dropped me back to midfield and then things really started to happen!

I set up Alexei Mikhailitchenko and from his cross, Gary scored with the header of his life. Then I got away again and big Mark netted with a diving header.

What a team Marseille were then. From Basile Boli at the back through Frank Sauzee and Marcel Desailly - who marked me in midfield - to Alen Boksic and Rudi Voller up front. They played us off the park that night.

Boli, of course, was to become an Ibrox team-mate and an interesting fella. Everyone thought it was a great signing but soon enough he made it clear in the French press that he wasn't enjoying it.

He hated the traditions, like always wearing a shirt and tie to training because that just doesn't happen in Europe. But it's part of the image of our club and I've never felt we should change it just for the foreigners.

But Baz didn't fancy it and fell foul of the manager by not wearing one a couple of times.

He got his own back one day and had us in stitches at training when he strode on to the park with the tracksuit on and silk tie still knotted around his neck! Near the end, though, the truth was he simply didn't want to play for Rangers and that was just a football thing.

It had nothing to do with religion, I swear. I'm supposed to have told Boli not to wear a cross under his jersey, but that is not true.

He was a Roman Catholic who often had his rosary beads with him in the dressing-room to help him - and that will shock some people.

Religion and football in Glasgow will always be linked but my main religion is being a Rangers man.

I don't go to church that often, but the Rev. Stewart Lamont still sees me from time to time at the Kinning Park church I used to go to with the BB. I'll take mum if she doesn't have a partner.

You can be painted as a bigot in a city like Glasgow, but I don't think it's fair to pin it on me. Yes, I've sung the songs on the terraces - and I'll come back and do it now I'm leaving.

I'm a Rangers man to my bones and I'm not ashamed of that. But that's as far as it goes.

Back on the field, our Euro run continued when we faced the unknown quantities of CSKA Moscow. The game was played in Bochum in Germany because of the severity of the Russian winter.

We somehow survived the most bizarre stramash of all time in the opening seconds when Davie Robertson kicked one off the line - and Ian Ferguson broke away to score a deflected goal as our luck held.

I reckon Fergie will definitely be the last Ranger to earn a testimonial and he deserves it. He has had his hard times at Ibrox, what with illness and injury, and has taken a lot of stick from the fans - but no one should ever question his commitment to the club.

His moaning is legendary. He's actually at his **HAPPIEST** when he's whingeing...if he didn't grump and groan in the morning you'd know something was wrong with him!

Next up, Bruges at home. They had a sneaky player called Lorenzo Stalens who conned big Mark into cuffing him round the ear just after I'd put us ahead and that was us down to ten men.

My emotions went from glee to woe in the blink of an eye because it had been a goal to remember.

Trevor Steven found me with a superb pass over what was a quagmire, one touch with the left and then a drilled shot low into the corner. What a feeling!

Then, of course, Scott Nisbet scored **THAT** *goal.*

It was more of a block tackle than a shot when he sent the ball flying in from out on the touchline in front of the dugout - but it hit a divot, spun over keeper Danny Verlinden and we won it 2-1.

Nissy got all the headlines. Typical.

His moment of glory shows you the luck we carried on that run. When you're a football player 10 or 15 per cent of your game can be governed by luck and we had it that year.

After Bruges at home, we faced them away and that was the game we should have won, the 90 minutes which should have helped us into the European Cup Final.

Everyone looks at Marseille away as our downfall, but in reality the draw we got there was a brilliant result.

No, for me it has always been down to that night in Belgium when we tied 1-1 because they were there for the taking.

Still, we were 90 minutes away from the European Cup Final. Victory over the French champions would put us in pole position - and I would have done anything to play in the Velodrome that night.

I had staples in my shinbone from an op, but had shaken one off and needed a painkilling injection. The ache in my leg was constant, it was giving me real grief.

But I talked Walter into playing me, begged him to let me take the jab. In the morning I only had a 30 percent chance but the needle worked. I was set on playing and I made it.

The walk down the corridor from the dressing rooms, deep in the dark bowels of the stadium, seemed endless. As we neared the end of the long trek, I always remember their president Bernard Tapie waiting at the mouth of the tunnel, urging his players on.

We were hurling insults at him. The atmosphere in that place was bonkers. Then they played Jump by Van Halen before the start and we were rocking. There were fireworks whizzing into the air as we walked out, it was an amazing sight.

Getting a win there was a daunting task, but I was standing shoulder to shoulder with men having the season of their lives.

Gough was a tower of strength, McCoist was to win the Golden Boot and McCall's will to win that year was astonishing - he was covering every blade of grass in every game.

And what can you say about Andy Goram that year? The Goalie is no angel, everyone knows that. But just give the guy a pair of gloves and let him out there and you're laughing.

He has his troubles, but I'll tell you why he has landed so many new deals at Gers - because he's the **BEST**. Simple as that.

People want to jump on the bandwagon and slaughter him for every little thing, but let them find a better keeper. Yet even *he* couldn't have stopped my shot that levelled Sauzee's opener that night - it was one of the hits of my life.

I remember big Boli trying to charge me down, but I ripped across the ball and it fizzed in. We were so close...yet at the end everyone knew deep down the chance had gone.

I always knew Marseille - who, remember, were later stripped of the cup in a bribes scandal - would get the result they needed in Bruges.

By hook or by crook...

As it turned out we could only draw 0-0 with CSKA at Ibrox. We missed chance after chance and I collapsed exhausted on the turf in utter dejection. The adventure was over.

I looked around and some players were half-heartedly trying to acknowledge the fans. Ally was in tears, Goughie had blood running down his face from yet another head wound. God, it really *was* over.

The Russians were running around celebrating the draw because they got £250,000 per point from UEFA. I thought: "Here I am, utterly bloody heartbroken, I'll never get this far in Europe again in my life and they're celebrating a draw!"

I lay there on the Ibrox turf in the midst of this bizarre scene, looked up into the night sky and thought back to that night in Marseille.

You see, I had a chance in the first-half and I should have hit it myself instead of trying to tee up Ally.

I know I should have hit it, I still see it in my mind's eye.

The way that season went for me it would probably have smacked into the net. But I passed the buck and even now it gets to me. I could have scored and it's haunted me ever since.

It will always be there, nagging away. We were one goal from glory.

CHAPTER 5

THE GOODISON, THE BAD AND THE UGLY

WHEN *you've played at the peaks of the Champions League, reserve football destroys you. That's what happened to Ian Durrant.*

The depth of the hurt was shown when he left his beloved Ibrox - albeit briefly - for a spell with English Premiership strugglers Everton.

Alongside £4.1m Rangers' misfit Duncan Ferguson - who had also made the journey south - Durrant was off on a new adventure.

It was to be the making of Ferguson but for Ian it became a soulsearching time, cut off from the footballing life-support machine that Ibrox had become.

He was exposed to a new lifestyle, a new football environment and a new understanding that not every manager operates to the scruples of Walter Smith.

ONE MONTH at Everton. It didn't sound long when they offered me it.

It sounded like a chance to get my head together and get my career back on track.

It sounded like a way out of the drudgery of reserve team football that was dragging my morale and self-belief lower and lower.

In truth, Everton for me was bittersweet. With a sour ending.

Yes, I loved my taste of the Premiership. But I got it with the wrong club - and will never forget how I was dumped in a **DISCO** by their manager Mike Walker.

Now, as I put the thoughts of a Rangers career down on paper, I'm at last getting used to the idea of life without the club. I've got to, because reserve football is no good to me at the age of 31. I can't handle it.

But any move will have to be the right move. Not like the day chairman David Murray told me Everton had been in for me and I just jumped at the first exit door I was offered.

I was going nowhere in the reserves and I was on a downer. Then in came Everton out of the blue. Maybe I should have thought about it more but I just said: "I'll give it a go."

There will be people in dead-end jobs reading this thinking I have nothing to complain about, that I'm a privileged footballer earning big money. And they're right in many ways.

But how do I explain how I felt back then? Maybe a couple of football terms will help. The reserves are called The Stiffs - as in dead men - or The Ham and Eggs, rhyming slang for The Dregs.

No one wants to feel they are the dregs, not in any job.

The odd moment apart - like the Old Firm second string games in front of 20,000 - those nicknames are just about spot-on.

Reserve football can be horrible when you have played at the heights as I have. It hurts your pride.

I've been skipper of the Rangers second eleven this last season, but inside you know you could be doing a turn in the first team. But there is this incredible squad there and you know you can't get in.

So I have been stuck and it has become soul-destroying because half the problem is it's too easy. You're there trying 80-yard balls and things you wouldn't dream of going for in a proper game.

You don't get the room to do that in the Premier League but even though teams will go man for man on me in the stiffs there's always space to indulge yourself. It's kid-on football at times.

Sometimes they are right good games and the fun of playing without real pressure reminds you of your youth. But on December afternoons at Creamery Park in Bathgate, where Rangers often play reserve games, there's no one watching and the wind is blowing you off your feet and you question why you are bothering.

From the Champions League to the reserves - it just shows you the highs and the lows of football.

I look at guys like Craig Moore and Charlie Miller - players who can be the mainstay of Rangers for years to come - and believe it's no use for them in the second team. You learn nothing there.

I've had so many lows in the second string, particularly going up to Aberdeen and taking pelters from their bitter fans because of the Neil Simpson incident.

You can hear every shout, ever narky comment and if as well as the abuse you lose then you're facing four miserable hours back down the road and the thought of creeping in to a dark house with Angela and the kids sleeping.

At quiet times like that I've sat in the TV lounge of my house and glanced away from the screen to the unit on which sits a small, framed picture of my Champions League goal against Ajax.

Okay, we lost 4-1 that night but the Amsterdam Arena is the sort of place where you dream of playing football and scoring goals.

You look at that snap and remember facing the likes of Marc Overmars and Patrick Kluivert and wonder what the point of your day has been.

You know when your brain begins to calm and you're ready for bed, you'll get up and be in training the next day and the motivation level is going to be zero.

Perhaps that explains why I was at such a low ebb back then. Sure, Everton are a big club and it could have been a great move, but really all I wanted at the time was a way out. Goodison provided it.

Yet if going south was to be an adventure of mixed emotions for me, it was the making of Duncan Ferguson.

I didn't even know the big man was going with me until we turned up at Ibrox and Walter Smith agreed to drive us down to Goodison to thrash out a deal.

Dunc, kept in the first team shadows by Mark Hateley despite his £4.1m price-tag from Dundee United, had signed for three months but I had a medical and they started having reservations.

I think their chairman Peter Johnson had been stung on a transfer with an injured player before, but I knew the records showed my knee was strong enough to survive the rigours of top class football again.

There had been talk of a £1.5m bid for me from them and I didn't feel I had anything to prove with my fitness. After all, I had played over 70 games in Scotland in the previous three seasons since coming back from the knee injury. Yet I also knew two or three players at Everton and things were going badly wrong at the time.

They had messed up moves for the Brazilian striker Muller and Chris Sutton and the fans were getting restless. I was even told Mike Walker had been overheard confessing: "I don't even know who these two Scottish guys are!"

So I was under no illusions about the sort of arena we were going into and that was confirmed when I went into the negotiations and I was told by Johnson that all they would offer was a month's trial.

Walter looked at me and said: "It's up to you."

I shrugged and said I'd go for it. I decided it was a chance to get my thinking straight and play first-team football again.

At Rangers I'd felt I was a man on a road to nowhere - but no one should make big decisions about their career on the spur of the moment. It's too important for that.

These days I have an agent in Blair Morgan who is shrewd in every area of football, contracts and the law and along with his consultants Trevor Steven and Steve Archibald - proven internationals who've seen and done it all - it means I have a wealth of experience to fall back on.

They act as a buffer and as I ponder my future now I can do it without being put in a predicament like I was back then. The Ian Durrant of old acted off the cuff and went to Goodison on a whim. I'm not so sure I would do the same now.

One thing's certain, I would thoroughly check on where I was going and on the coach in charge.

I walked into a very unhappy club at Everton. There was constant bickering in the dressing-room and the bulk of the players weren't happy. It made me yearn for Ibrox.

The whole feeling around the place wasn't helped by the fact that at their training ground the first team change in three different dressing-rooms instead of all being together.

I think it created a hierarchy and there were definitely cliques. I'll never forget walking in for the first day and Paul Rideout, an old Ibrox pal, said: "Jesus Christ Durranty, what the **** are you doing here? Do you realise the state we're in?"

The first they knew about the two of us coming down was when they read it in the papers and he was shocked that I had left Rangers to come to this utter mess.

I told Paul I was only trying to get my head together. But I think deep down right from the off I felt it was a bad idea. I realised pretty damn quick this might be a club under pressure, a club with problems.

The cold, hard truth is that I wanted to come home after two days but I was to walk away from that club after my month with more experience in the bank and little regard for Mike Walker. It would perhaps shock you to know that when I walked onto the training pitch, Walker's first words to me were: "Where do you play, son?"

Here I was just, two years after all the glory of the Champions League with 11 caps for my country and - hopefully - still loved by the Rangers fans and this guy didn't know me from Adam. *Take that.*

I almost said left-back. But instead I told him the truth and observed a manager under the cosh walk off with some new knowledge.

He was feeling the heat because he had spent a whole lot of money on players who simply weren't doing it. Dunc and I were the last throw of the dice in many ways...trouble is the chairman was holding his dice.

Walker, in fact, was a man I never really saw a lot of. It was generally the former Wales No.2 Dave Williams who would coach us. Still, there was a fresh challenge ahead and the promise of a first team chance which was more than was on offer at Ibrox at the time.

My Everton jersey still hangs in a room that has my pool table in it at home and if I'm lining up a shot I'll glance up and look at "Durrant 20" on the back.

It is an unfamiliar strip to bear my name and it was strange to play for a club other than Rangers. Yet it was a worthwhile experience.

I feel I had a good spell down there, even though they were struggling badly, and in a strange way it gave me some confidence in myself again.

Yet I remember being on the bench in my first match in the Coca-Cola Cup at Portsmouth, who had my old Celtic rival Gerry Creaney in their side, and we got knocked out.

I was running up and down, warming up for about 15 minutes and Walker never gave me a sniff. I was thinking: "What the bloody hell have I let myself in for here?"

I eventually pulled a different club's shirt on for the first time in my pro career in a 2-0 defeat by Southampton at The Dell. Still, at least the jersey was blue!

Walker was under pressure that day and once more I was a sub but there was hope on the bench when they lost Bruce Grobelaar with a bust cheekbone in the first few minutes.

Big Dave Beasant was slung in but we hardly had a shot and the Saints went ahead through Ronnie Ekelund.

At half-time I was still looking at Walker and waiting for the nod and he decided to put me on to try and spark things. I felt I did OK, but Matt Le Tissier - who else? - killed us off. We were stone last in the table.

Inside, though, I felt good about myself again. I always knew I could play in the Premiership and I'd proved it in that short spell. Or at least I thought I had.

I definitely don't regret going because they had some decent players to learn little things from. Guys like Daniel Amokachi, who'd been with Bruges when we faced them in the Champions League.

I was to come back with a resolve inside me to eventually get back into the Rangers team and into the Scottish Cup Final squad.

The football, in fact, was very enjoyable. We were second bottom when Dunc and I went and had climbed six places by the time I left so I like to think we did something to help.

Duncan Ferguson and controversy have walked hand in hand since he once ended up with a pay packet of £12-a-week at Dundee United because Jim McLean was fining him so much.

Now he's Public Enemy No.1 in Scotland because of his letter to the SFA counting himself out of playing for the international team in the future. There are those who say "Good riddance" and for the life of me I just can't understand that.

Ask any defender who has faced Ferguson in full flight and they will tell you that when he's up for the cup in a match he is frightening.

That's why I'm so saddened by his decision not to play for Scotland again. I wish he would change his mind.

The roots of all the bitterness, of course, lie in his jail sentence after the headbutt on Raith Rovers' John McStay in an otherwise routine 4-0 win at Ibrox. It was to cost him 44 days of his life in Barlinnie Prison.

I've been very close to the big man and I've seen him go through a lot. From the McStay incident to the troubles off the park when he was charged by the law - everything was heaping on to him.

He was already living with the pressure of that £4.1million price tag at Rangers at such a young age and I feel he found it all hard to live up to.

I never tried to visit him in the Bar-L because the message was put out by Dunc to the players that he simply wanted to get his head down and do his time.

Imagine what he went through. Think about it for a second, try and forget whatever your personal feelings are about the guy. Doesn't it scare you that you can be nicked for things that happen on a football field? It sure scares me.

Football should govern itself, but you can look back to that day and think that if the ref Kenny Clark had been harsher and red-carded Dunc none of this would have happened. Who knows?

There was a public outcry and everyone said Rangers were getting away with it all and a whole storm was whipped up.

That's why Duncan feels injustice at what happened to him in Scotland and football-wise it's a sad indictment on our game that we've lost him. He's got so much to offer and I've seen other sides to Dunc that would surprise you after the way he is portrayed.

For instance, when we were holed up in the Moat House in Liverpool I found hotel life difficult - and I'm supposed to be the confident one. Dunc just seemed to draw strength from it.

I discovered then that he's a very deep boy, sensitive even. We'd go down to dinner some nights and chat and that would be the only time he'd speak to you for three days. I'm different. I need my friends and family around me. At Everton I was on the phone every day to Ally to have some banter and catch up on the Ibrox gossip.

I also missed Angela a lot and she ended up coming down to stay for a spell, but hated it. God knows how I'd have coped if we'd had the kids then and I was marooned away from them.

But all the time Duncy was coping well. Sure, he'd have something on his mind and his way of coping is keeping it all inside himself.

We talked a lot about what went wrong at Rangers and he always told me how much it hurt him, he felt he'd failed at Ibrox.

He's a big Rangers man from a big Rangers family and all he wanted to do was play for the club. He did that but he never really fulfilled what he could have been because Hateley was playing so well.

Duncan let himself down off the park and it killed him at Gers. In the end he had to leave Glasgow.

At the start down in Liverpool he was saying to me: "Durranty, this is just three months. I'll get myself together, get some first-team football under my belt and then prove myself at Rangers."

There was no use having a £4.1m striker on the bench or in the reserves at Ibrox and the loan deal made sense. Big Mark had sniffed the threat and was playing out of his skin and in the end we lost Dunc which is a big regret for me.

I feel Duncan Ferguson is the most complete centre-forward British football has to offer alongside Alan Shearer.

He has so much skill as well as his famed aerial power and I feel Walter would have loved to have put him in right away. But with Mark's form he just couldn't justify it.

He tried to play them together and that was never going to work because two big men get in each other's way. Each needs a forager like McCoist beside them.

Eventually, Hateley's brilliance meant Dunc was gone and now look at him. He's a **GOD** down there yet at the time I remember he just seemed pleased to be out of the goldfish bowl existence there is as a Rangers player in Glasgow.

The most interesting thing of all for me at Everton was watching Dunc transform himself from this player who had seemed harried and worried at times at Gers. He fancied this.

I remember we played Arsenal at Goodison and he was incredibly wound-up because he wanted to show Tony Adams what he was made of. He did too. He battered Adams that day, dominated him. That was supposedly the best centre-half in Britain and Dunc showed him up.

David Unsworth scored that day in a 1-1 draw and it was my best game for the club, a memorable occasion for us all round.

I actually had a good rapport with the Everton fans, although it seemed strange playing in front of another set of supporters after all Rangers had come to mean to me.

Dunc, meanwhile, was on a different level. From that duel against Adams and Arsenal, the Everton fans took to him because there is a big aura about the No.9 jersey at that club.

From Joe Royle to Bob Latchford to Andy Gray, legends have been created in it. Now it holds another in the making.

We were Rangers men away from home, though, and I'll always remember when we beat West Ham 1-0 in a midweek game there was a huge contingent of Gers fans there.

I had four home games with Everton and the Bears were always there. My family liked the novelty of watching me play for someone else too - and the support from back home meant the world to Fergie and me.

It's great to see him with the responsibility of the Everton captaincy now and the way he has risen to that. He's getting married and if he ever returned to Scotland he would come back a wiser and stronger man.

I know in my heart that a lot of his problems came because he was naive and he couldn't handle that massive price tag. I felt sorry for him. He should have been a Rangers' great and it's sad because Gers fans haven't seen Duncan Ferguson at his best.

I swapped tops with Dunc when we played them in a pre-season friendly and I still pray that one day I'll see him in the **REAL** blue again, Rangers blue.

In reality, though, he's signed a long-term deal down there and he even has an Everton **TATTOO**. I said he was deep - but he's still daft!

If he ever sits down to write a book like this, Everton will be his life story. For me it's just a chapter and it had no happy ending.

There was competition for my position. Vinny Samways was similar in style to me and they started making noises about a kid in the reserves called Tony Grant.

The writing was on the wall after the West Ham game. My month was up and a couple of my team-mates asked me in the bath what the future was. But I didn't know - and I had to find out.

I waited around for the word from Walker but nothing happened and so I went to off a disco with some pals from Glasgow who had travelled down for the game.

Who should be there in a place called the Continental Club but Mike Walker. This was it, time to settle the issue. I walked over and said: "My month's up, can you tell me. Is there anything happening?"

He said: "No, I've decided I'm not keeping you on."

That was it - game over.

If he was any sort of man at all he would have taken me aside after the game and told me what the score was instead of trying to put on a show in front of his friends.

He was there in company and they could see me talking to him. I knew what the topic of conversation would be when he returned to his table.

I picked up the *Daily Record* when I came up the road to read Walker saying: "When you've got a homegrown youngster coming through you don't want to block his progress.

"Ian has done nothing wrong, he played well and was a big influence in the dressing-room. But I only ever wanted him on loan to have a look at him. We've let the player know where he stands."

They did that alright - but those nice words weren't said to my face. I just got a dismissive brush-off in that disco.

The whole episode opened my eyes up but I got a boost from the Gaffer immediately when he put me in the squad for the game with Partick Thistle and hoisted my spirits.

I'd been used to honesty and dignity like that from Walter - Mike Walker could learn a lesson from him.

CHAPTER 6

NINE IN A ROW

IT was fate that when the most important game in Rangers' history rolled around they would fall back on one of their favourite sons, a man who knew just what nine-in-a-row meant to the club.

For Ian Durrant, March 16, 1997 against Celtic was a date with destiny and he was to play a key role in securing three priceless points in a 1-0 win at Parkhead as Walter Smith's side marched towards that fabled record.

Even for a battle-hardened Old Firm veteran this was the game of his life in the most tension-packed season the club has ever had to endure.

The fans know the war of nerves they suffered through before the sense of release when that ninth crown was finally clinched with Brian Laudrup's header at Tannadice. But what was it like behind the scenes at Ibrox?

Here Ian takes us inside the camp during one of the most significant seasons in 125 years of Rangers.

I WOKE up in the hotel room and the depression hit home. It was one of the biggest days Rangers had ever seen and in my heart of hearts I felt there was no way I would be playing.

Five hours later the side to face Celtic in the mother of all Old Firm games was named and I was walking on air.

Walter Smith's eyes scanned a grim-faced bunch of players in a hotel team-meeting. Then he said the following words: **Dibble, Cleland, Albertz, Gough, McLaren, Bjorklund, Moore, Ferguson, DURRANT!, Hateley and Laudrup.**

The 11 players to face the Parkhead crunch and, for me, the team who truly won us nine-in-a-row.

Alright, there were flutters and scares on the closing straight, but **THAT** was the win which eventually saw us match Celtic's historic record of successive title triumphs. Don't let anyone tell you different.

I was the boy from nowhere. It was my first start for four months. But when it mattered I was in. And the news turned my world on its head.

I'd even set up to watch the game in the hotel room with the injured Andy Goram, because sitting among the crowd at Parkhead with the Rangers blazer on is not the best experience in the world.

I told the Goalie I'd go through the formality of the team-meeting then bell him and watch it in the safety of the room. That team-meeting was anything but a formality, though. I was playing.

As usual through all my time at Gers I was rooming with Coisty but there hadn't been as much banter as normal in the build-up.

Injuries meant we were in a state of emergency and the Gaffer had gone to QPR to bring Mark Hateley back. It was clear the old warhorse was a cert to play. Ally knew that meant he was a sub and that was hard for both of us to take, because I believed the bench was the best I could hope for too.

That's where I'd been stuck in the Scottish Cup game with Celtic ten days earlier when we lost 2-0 and I only got on to buzz around for the last ten minutes.

Even in that little spell, though, Walter must have spotted something there in me, a desire to prove something. Whatever it was, I was in and looking back perhaps it was because he knew how much the games against Celtic mean to me.

Let me say it again. I would never see myself as a bigot. I'm just a Rangers man through and through and proud of it.

There are men like me at both clubs, although with the growing influx of foreigners that devoted band is dwindling.

I always fought with Peter Grant on the pitch, but there was always respect there. If we weren't playing in those matches I'd have been at one end singing my songs and he'd have been at the other singing his.

70

The bottom line is that when Old Firm games come round there is no motivation needed, it takes care of itself. And on that Sunday in March I was in the middle of the biggest Old Firm game of my life.

We were under pressure because we simply hadn't played in the cup game and had been caned. We owed the fans after that.

Yet I've never felt so confident about winning as I did that day. I hared out to make a call to my missus Angela and my mum to say I'd leave tickets for them.

And then I could settle, knowing they were there watching me when it really mattered. I've played in some atmospheres in my life, seen some sights but that day topped it all.

It was **BEDLAM**, far beyond anything even I have experienced in 14 years of Old Firm games.

You went to take a throw-in and you could feel pure hatred raining down on you from the Celtic fans - and I'm sure it was the same for their players when they came near our lot.

That's the way Old Firm games affect people, but this time it all got too much. The overpowering hype **OFF** the field before that match turned the 90 minutes **ON** it into a **FARCE**.

It was an awful game to play in and even when I've watched the video of it I've sat there in disbelief. Ever since Souness drummed it into me, I've always prided myself on the value of possession.

I don't think I've ever given the ball away so much in my life as I did in that one game.

Yes, it was a dreadful advert for football. But you know what? I don't really care. What mattered was the result.

And it was a game that shows how players from outside Scotland simply can't handle the Rangers-Celtic confrontations at times.

My case for the prosecution? Paolo di Canio.

He lost the plot that day. I'm a fan of his and I'm afraid I had to give him a couple of slaps early on in that game simply because I couldn't catch him. He really is a fantastic footballer.

He started so well and bewildered us with a few tricks without really getting at us, before he battered the bar with an unbelievable volley from a free-kick that was flicked up for him.

Yet for all that mesmerising skill, Paolo is a guy who lets himself down when he gets involved in so many stupid arguments. I mean, earlier that season he got himself sent off before the ball was centred after **HE'D** scored a penalty against Hearts.

There were incidents involving Paolo throughout that game and they weren't pretty. He made a snapping gesture at Ian Ferguson and told him he was going to break his leg.

Fergie told him he'd see him in the tunnel and although di Canio was

71

going bonkers at the end and trying to get to Ian they never met again.

I have to say I know who I would back.

Paolo's anger came after a game that had plenty of drama, even if it had no skill - and I was to be at the centre of it all.

We edged ahead from a long ball from Jorg Albertz. I gave Alan Stubbs a little sly tug to win myself a yard and I was away down the left. I remember looking up and wondering what the hell their keeper Stewart Kerr was doing out there and then lobbing over him.

I still don't know to this day what Malky Mackay was thinking about either as the ball headed for goal. I've always felt he should have dived and headed it away, but I'm glad he didn't.

Lauders appeared to get a touch and he got the credit, but whatever happened and whoever you think scored that goal it won Nine-in-a-Row and I know I played a part. That's good enough for me.

Of course, it couldn't end there because Old Firm games never do. There had to be controversy.

And - apart from Paolo losing his marbles - the big debate came with a red card for big Mark. Welcome home.

He got involved in a clash with Mackay and before we knew where we were Kerr had lost the place and come racing out of his goal to mix it. For me it was handbags at ten paces as he came out swinging.

I remember Charlie Miller was trying to hold him back from big Mark - and I have to say I was thinking: "Let him go for it!"

Ref Hugh Dallas was under enormous pressure in that match and when Mark got involved I knew he would go. Now we were under the cosh, but we survived and there has seldom been a sweeter sound than the final whistle that day. Even then the rows weren't over as we mocked the Celtic huddle and celebrated in style!

Maybe that was a case of us letting our hearts rule our heads but they did one **AFTER** the cup game and, believe me, we never forgot that.

None of us minded the huddle **BEFORE** the game if that's their trademark, but afterwards it felt like rubbing your nose in it.

When you're a Glasgow boy like me you are hurting enough when you lose that game without that sort of stuff going on.

So we gave as good as we'd got and before we knew it we were the subject of an SFA enquiry. I've seen things blown out of proportion before, but that was ridiculous.

Still, this is the one game that never fails to get everyone's vision out of perspective. For days afterwards I was maintaining that it was a good match to play in - yet I've watched it since and it was appalling.

In the dressing-room afterwards, we knew deep down we had won the title yet the manager was very subdued and it wasn't until later that I truly understood why.

I think there were just so many feelings bubbling under the surface that he didn't trust himself to let them out in case he lost his dignity.

Archie Knox was going round saying: "Do you see the finish line? Can you smell the hot dogs?"

Walter? he was treating it as just another win. Me? Well, I was going **BERSERK**! Mark was sitting with his shoulders slumped, shaking his head muttering over and over: "I can't believe I was sent off".

He was disconsolate, but soon everyone lifted his spirits and the party started. We had a couple of beers in the showers and then - despite all the hype and all the hatred that day - we went into the Players' Lounge for a drink after the game.

Their players were understandably dejected and hadn't surfaced as quickly as us but the welcome from the Celtic staff couldn't have been warmer. There's still a mutual respect between the two clubs and it was there that day even with the stakes as high as they get.

That's why it disappointed me in the aftermath that everyone tried to focus on things we'd supposedly done in the Parkhead dressing-room.

Much was made of us having a picture of the Queen in there, but the truth is the picture goes everywhere with kit-man Jimmy Bell.

It goes up in the dressing-room whether it's Parkhead or Pittodrie.

There's also a framed picture of the Queen in the home dressing-room at Ibrox too and it's sour grapes to suggest we had it at Parkhead that day to wind anyone up.

It's nothing to do with bigotry for me, just an acknowledgment of the roots of our club. I was born and raised a Rangers fan and I still think players who know what the jersey really means count for a lot in Old Firm games. There will be critics shaking their heads and saying how narrow-minded I am when they read that, but what can I say?

You haven't been out there in the heat of it all - that's why I say that you're better playing Scottish players in Old Firm games. They truly understand it.

Look at di Canio that day, look at Gazza when he was caught playing the imaginary flute as he warmed up at the 1998 New Year derby at Celtic Park .

Sure, there are other factors at work in those cases. Paolo saw the title disappearing over the horizon and every little thing Paul does is under so much scrutiny.

He made that gesture for two seconds, got caught and all hell broke loose. I'm scared to fart in live Sky games because they've got so many cameras!

But there's a serious point here. Gascoigne is a hugely talented boy but he gets caught up in it all. He reacts in bad situations where Ally or I might take things with a pinch of salt.

Sure, Gazza loves Rangers - but he wasn't *born* with Rangers. There's a different kind of understanding there. There have been exceptional foreigners in the past few years like Laudrup and, yes, di Canio.

You cherish the day they signed because they bring so much more skill to the fixture. But I have sat and watched imports in our dressing-room and their eyes are popping out of their heads before the Celtic game.

Our Danish striker Erik Bo Andersen is an example of both sides of the coin. Erik came from Aalborg for £1.4m and went back home to Odense with a remarkable ratio of 15 goals in 23 starts.

He was incredibly quick but the point about him in one Old Firm game is that he **FORGOT** what he was good at, he forgot his pace was his big asset. He came off the bench and scored two goals in a 3-1 win at New Year on the way to nine-in-a-row and he'll never be forgotten for that.

But he also played in the cup game from the start and he just couldn't handle it. You just don't get the time to even bring the ball down in Old Firm games and there was Erik trying to take touches here and there and getting caught in possession every time.

He eventually left the field with a fractured skull that night which was a harsh penalty I wouldn't wish on anyone - but it all came down to being involved in a game he couldn't cope with.

Don't listen to those coaches who talk nonsense about just another three points. This isn't just another game.

We talk about people having the balls - in other words the courage - to play when it counts. Well, you need the balls of a rhinoceros to play in an Old Firm game.

It's sad in some ways. You lose and you're going into hiding for a week which is hard on your family. And that's the truth, not an exaggeration. You'll go into training, have a quiet spot of lunch then go home.

You are, after all, a man who has let down half of Glasgow and your first thought is a visit to Skellys to ask if they've got any bulletproof motors in stock!

The run-in to Nine, of course, wasn't without its hiccups. Six days after that win over Celtic we lost 2-1 at home to Killie and I was back on the bench for a 4-0 win over Dunfermline - then bombed out when we won 6-0 at Raith to move a huge step closer.

I was back on the bench, though, for the sellout Nine-in-a-Row party. Or at least it was *meant* to be a party...shame someone forgot to tell our visitors from Motherwell!

There we were with the hats on and the champers chilling and we got dumped 2-0 in front of a full house at our place.

To make matters worse, I came on and tripped up Mickey Weir for Owen Coyle to score the penalty that clinched it. But if that was a bad dream, what happened next was my worst nightmare.

I don't know if I can put into words what winning the ninth title meant to guys like Coisty and myself, the fans who became players for Rangers.

All our lives we'd dreamed of a night like the one that loomed at Tannadice on May 7, 1997 when a win would put our names in the history books.

Once again the team went up and I was stood staring at it in shock and dismay. I wasn't there. Not even on the bench.

A lump came to my throat and I don't mind admitting that tears were welling up in my eyes.

All I ever wanted was to be on that park the day we won Nine-in-a-Row, it was an emotional thing for me. But I'm afraid emotions don't come into it at Rangers.

I suppose no manager can pick a team on his feelings - quite rightly, they must pick teams to win.

But forget the injury, forget missing 30 months of my career, forget days when we've lost to Celtic. Being dropped for that night at Tannadice hurt me more than anything in my 14 years at Rangers.

Ally was there on the bench alongside Jorg Albertz - who'd started most of the games that season - and I was genuinely happy for Derek McInnes to be involved as a sub because he is another who really does love the club.

But the bottom line is that I missed out and it hurt like Hell.

When you arrive at a ground and you're not playing, you're at a loss.

If it's a home game you have your two complimentary tickets to leave at the door and maybe Bob Reilly, the Commercial Manager, will ask you in to meet some sponsors up in the Executive Suites.

Those are all little tasks you can busy yourself with to dodge the hard fact that you've been dropped. But away from home you're a lost soul and you just want the game to start.

There are corporate boxes just above the tunnel in the corner of Tannadice and I sat in there with the rest of the unwanted and the injured. There's an empty feeling when you're stuck there, you don't feel part of it. I was there with Barry Ferguson - who will win plenty of titles with Rangers in the future - Seb Rozental and Goughie.

For Barry and Seb it was different. Fergie obviously comes from a Rangers family but he's just setting out on his Gers' career. Seb had cost us £3.8m from Chile but has been so unlucky with injuries and hasn't played enough to get a true feeling for the club.

Goughie? Well, it meant everything to him. Just like me.

We leapt up together like any other Rangers' punters when Charlie Miller swept over a brilliant cross and Lauders flew in with the header.

It was a picture-book ball and a header from a guy who practices that very skill four times a season! What a goal, what a way to clinch it!

But the sorry fact is that I was sat in a stand in a blazer. I didn't have my working clothes on.

Yet you have to choke back that hurt pride and smile, be happy for the club. That wasn't hard because at last we'd done it.

The manager took us for a few drinks at the Swallow Hotel on the way out of Dundee on the way home - just as Graeme Souness had seven years before. We had champers then, of course.

Those were mad scenes. Gazza trooped across the car park from the bus for a drink still wearing his strip and the drive home flew past.

It only seemed like 10 minutes and then we came through George Square where the fans were having a street party. It was pandemonium.

Celtic supporters had their own Nine-in-a-Row heroes and when I was a young kid that was all they talked about. You envied them.

Now we had emulated that and I hope that players like Ally McCoist, Ian Ferguson and Richard Gough - the three players who have played in **EVERY** Nine-in-a-Row season - are remembered as legends like those Celtic boys. They should be.

As for me, injury counted me out of playing in the Nine, of course. But I've never told anyone that I actually am a member of that elite club.

In a private moment in the dark days of the injury Graeme Souness came to me and gave me the medal I missed out on. I know in my heart I never played the games but the medals mean the world to me.

I was back in for the final game at Hearts when we lost 3-1 before returning to Ibrox for the party to begin but the hard pro in me told me that was a meaningless match. When it mattered I was missing in action.

Yet even now I can't bring myself to blame Walter or bear a grudge against him. I actually feel it may have been harder for him not to play me than it was for me to stomach the decision. His heart may have told him to put me on the bench but if his head said to leave me out then what he did was right.

We've never spoken about it and this is the first time I ever have - and ever will - speak about my feelings that night in public.

I swallowed my pride, I put on a brave face and I joined in the celebrations because the club has always been what matters most to me.

Yet I won't pretend that I was happy inside myself. Walter Smith has done more for me in my life than I could ever recount in a book.

But that night he broke my heart.

CHAPTER 7

THE MAGNIFICENT SEVEN

THERE is a glass-fronted cabinet in Ian Durrant's Bothwell home that reflects on his role as a Cup Final talisman for Rangers.

Inside are seven medals from seven finals with the club and they're ALL winner's medals.

Think of it. Seven Finals in one Rangers career, the law of averages says you must lose some time but not Durrant.

Instead he won three Man of the Match awards in those games and proved that he deserves the reputation he has always carried. The man for the big occasion.

Here he reflects on a decade of glory in Scottish football's showpiece games - from the day when Davie Cooper stole the show to the match that will always be thought of as The Laudrup Final.

No.1: Skol Cup Rangers 2 Celtic 1, Hampden, October 22, 1986
Scorers: Rangers: Durrant, Cooper (pen) Celtic: McClair

IT was Graeme Souness' first Cup Final and to get him off to a flyer like that really made his era at Rangers. Four months in the job and he could point to silverware in the trophy-room to justify the chairman David Holmes' faith in him.

That was a simmering match and it just shows how the Old Firm atmosphere affects people when you think of the ref Davie Syme at Hampden.

He'd been walloped on the back of the head - by a 50p thrown from the crowd - and he somehow decided that Celtic's midfielder Tony Shepherd had punched him.

Up went the red card and Tony was off. He was going potty trying to prove his innocence and I was standing in the centre circle giggling!

Then Syme suddenly saw sense and order was restored as Tony stayed on. But it was one of those mayhem matches.

I've spoken about the action of this Final elsewhere but one thing really dominates my thoughts when I go back now - Mo Johnston lost the place completely.

He tried to stick the head on Stuart Munro and then on the spur of the moment he crossed himself on the way off the park. You couldn't have imagined that one day he'd be a Rangers player!

I've got pals in the District Bar who never forgave him for that and I never took him in there, he stayed in Edinburgh well away from all the hassle of Glasgow.

As for the players it was forgotten the minute Souness signed him as our first high-profile Catholic player - although Mo did have to win his spurs behind the scenes.

When he arrived at our training camp at Il Ciocco in the Tuscany Hills he found one table set with bread and water for one person in the corner in the players' dining-room. Thanks to Coisty.

Ally had known Mo was signing for us and been sworn to secrecy and was already won over but our kitman Jimmy Bell wasn't.

He laid your training gear outside your room each morning and handed out the special privileges of chocolate brought from home.

There would be Coisty's kit with two packets of Maltesers on top of it and a couple of bars of Dairy Milk. What did Mo get? Nothing.

He had a long job winning Jimmy over.

No.2: Skol Cup Rangers 3 Aberdeen 3, Hampden October 25, 1987
Rangers won 5-3 on pens after extra-time
Scorers: Rangers: Cooper, Durrant, Fleck Aberdeen: Bett, Falconer, Hewitt

THIS was one of the greatest games I ever played for Rangers, everything I tried came off.

I was trying things I wouldn't have dreamed of and I still watch the video of that Final to this day. I'll sit in my TV room and look at it and it still thrills me. What a game.

And the goal ranks as one of my all-time best for the club too. It came off their throw-in and I won it to work a 1-2 with Robert Fleck before Ally slipped me in with a superb little flick.

Now I was one on one with Jim Leighton, such an accomplished keeper, but I was having one of those days where the goals look huge.

I steered it into the corner with the outside of my right foot and I was off and running.

I have great satisfaction when I look back at it these days and see the reaction it brought from Walter Smith. He was running around the Hampden track punching the air.

If you look at it closely there's this separated at birth thing with McCoist. I'm just about to shoot and he's away at the side of the box mimicking me, kicking thin air!

We always had great Finals with Aberdeen at that time and this was a classic. We were actually 3-2 down with just four minutes left and Fleckie pushed me out the way to score an equaliser that I have to admit now had more than a hint of offside about it.

We pummelled them in extra-time but we just couldn't score and it was on to penalties.

Souness and Smith were out with the list and it read: McCoist, Fleck, Francis, Cooper and Durrant. I was last and I was ready.

They had Jim Bett, Peter Weir, John Hewitt, Willie Miller and Peter Nicholas. I looked at their faces and we were taking the kicks into the Rangers End. I was confident, everything had come off for me and there was no way I was missing.

Coop was pacing around and he came up to me and said: "Do you know what you're doing with it, son?"

I replied: "Aye, it's going in the pokey."

The fans had heart attacks as Trevor Francis scored off a one-step run-up but that was his style.

Sure enough, Nicholas smacked one off the bar and over to miss for them and it came down to me to score to win the Cup.

It felt like a Sunday park game because I was flying so high and I just side-footed it low into Leighton's left-hand corner and set off to celebrate. The photographers followed and I couldn't get to the Rangers End without vaulting over them in a single bound like Superman - which I'd probably have got away with that day!

Instead I just turned and waited for Coisty and Jimmy Nicholl to get to me. Partying in front of our fans was the perfect end to a perfect day.

You know, I look at myself running away to celebrate that day and I look so young and vibrant I wish for a time machine to take me back there.

I remember lying in the team bath with Coisty and we had a bottle of champagne each. With the mixture of bubbly and adrenalin we were blitzed at the Press conference!

No.3: Tennents Scottish Cup Rangers 2 Airdrieonians 1
Hampden, May 9 1992
Scorers: Rangers: Hateley, McCoist Airdrie: Smith

WE'D waited 11 years to bring the Scottish Cup back to Rangers and one word sums up this match. Tension.

I thought the best I could hope for this day was a sub's jersey but I landed a role wide on the right, not my favourite.

We walked out in our new Adidas kit for the first time and looked good as we cruised two up through Mark and Ally.

But big Andy Smith battered one into the top corner with five minutes left and all of a sudden it was a war of nerves.

Yet we made it and the performance was forgotten because we had the trophy back for the first time since Coop had inspired the team to a 4-1 replay win over Dundee United in 1981.

And when you've won a Final with Rangers there's no better feeling than coming back to Ibrox and showing the Cup round the local pubs including the Rangers Supporters' Club and, of course, The District Bar.

Then the Ibrox doors are shut and the Rangers family gets down to party. Ally's pal Cliff Smith has a band called Cartel who are excellent and they've entertained us a few times.

I have to say my pal Coisty is some chanter. He goes through the Springsteen book then blows you away with Eric Clapton's *Knocking on Heaven's Door*.

And we've found another couple of turns in recent years - Derek McInnes with Guns and Roses' *Sweet Child of Mine* and the Gaffer.

Yes, I can reveal that Walter Smith wrecks his image and tortures *Hey Jude* or any other number by the Beatles the band can remember.

No.4 Skol Cup Rangers 2 Aberdeen 1
Hampden, October 25, 1992
Scorers: Rangers: McCall, Smith OG Aberdeen: Shearer

THIS game came amidst a glut of matches for us but we coped to edge it and you'll never find a more delighted scorer than McCall.

The passback rule had just come in then and Theo Snelders tried to chest one down and bulleted it back out eight yards to Stuart for a tap-in.

When Theo signed for us I was in the dressing-room thumping his torso and he said in that Dutch accent: "Wee man, what are you doing?"

I said: "Don't worry, I'm just checking for that steel plate you had in your chest in the Skol Cup Final!"

That wasn't the most memorable of Finals but it was the first leg of a Treble on the board when David Robertson's cross caught Gary Smith out and he stretched for the header and sent it skidding past Snelders.

No.5 Tennents Scottish Cup Rangers 2 Aberdeen 1
Parkhead, May 29, 1993
Scorers: Rangers: Murray, Hateley Aberdeen: Richardson

OUT of the seven Cup Finals I played for Rangers I won the lot and also walked away with three Man of the Match awards. I quite liked the big time.

This was another day when I felt I hit form and when I look back to these Finals I realise now with the benefit of hindsight that Walter Smith was waging psychological warfare all the time and I was the victim.

In the build-up to these games I'd often be on tenterhooks thinking I was destined for the bench and it was like that before this one.

I'd been out for three weeks and Gary McSwegan had been banging in a few goals but then at our pre-match camp at Turnberry I was called to Walter's room to hear the magic words: "You're playing tomorrow. I need you."

That was the end of a season that had brought a 44-game unbeaten run, that great European campaign, Ally's broken leg and now the chance of the Treble.

We had been through it all but we found the resolve from somewhere to go ahead with Neil Murray's deflected shot before I set up Hateley for one of those goals he bludgeoned in on the run with that hammer left peg.

Lee Richardson pulled one back and we were on our last legs in the last 10 minutes but we made it. That team always did.

We had a great year that season but at the end it was a team living simply on that dream of winning the Treble at Parkhead of all places.

That was the ultimate for me.

The following year we could have won back to back Trebles but Dundee United scuppered that in the Scottish Cup Final. This, though, was THE season.

Everything just blended because we were so close together and I think the manager would admit he's spent the five years since trying to emulate that team.

Even then just playing in the game wasn't enough for me as far as Ally was concerned. He'd been away the night before and forgotten to pack his stuff for a slot on the TV panel for the Final.

So I had to get Angela to bring in a blue jacket, white shirt, blue tie and a pair of trousers for him. He should be proud to this day that my strides fitted him.

He hobbled about his crutches and emotionally bit the bullet that day - just as I had so often in the past - and smiled for the team. I knew how he felt being out of it.

No.6 League Cup Rangers 2 Hibernian 1
Celtic Park, October 24, 1993
Scorers: Rangers: Durrant, McCoist Hibernian: McPherson OG.

THIS was the Roy of the Rovers Final.

I scored and won Man of the Match and my best friend came off the bench to make his comeback from a leg break and grabbed the winner with an overhead kick. All this on the turf of our greatest rivals. Honestly, you couldn't script it.

It was my first goal in Scottish football over two months into the season - I'd been on target in Europe - and Ally's first of any description. What a time to score them.

Yet that day it had come down to a simple choice for Walter Smith. Durrant OR McCoist to start.

Ally had been back from his broken leg for three games and he felt he was fit. But Walter, always aware of how close we are to each other, made sure he pulled us aside together in the dressing-room.

He said: "Ally, you're not ready yet. I'm going with Durranty."

Coisty wasn't happy and it was a strange twist for me to feel great that I was in the 11 yet heart-sorry for my pal who was being handed a tracksuit.

I lifted the opener over Jim Leighton and sparked another betting coup for the Durrant family who were all on me for first goal at 12-1. Will those bookies never learn?

But Dave McPherson decided to do his Big Bird out of Sesame Street impersonation in the middle of our goals and got those legs all fankled

BABY BLUES...lapping up a goal in my debut season,
everything seemed so simple back then!

*PAUL THE RAGE...Celtic's Paul McStay - one of the best I
ever played beside for Scotland - grits his teeth and starts
the chase in my Old Firm debut in 1985*

*SCARF ACE...the colours are raised in the air and I'm
telling the Enclosure just how much I've enjoyed the
winner against Celtic in August 1986. I gave Coop the
biggest rubber ear ever in the celebrations!*

SKOL SMILES…another trophy in the bag and skipper Terry Butcher leads the party after we beat Celtic 2-1 in the Final to give Souness his first trophy in 1986

SCORE ON THE DOORS…20 up for the young Durrant and Stuart Munro and Ted McMinn give me a lift. My hair is under control by now but what about Cammy Fraser's moustache??

BUDDIE SYSTEM…shielding possession from Ian Ferguson when he was at St Mirren. He would become a close Ibrox pal after his £1m move

BEST OF ENEMIES…yet again Fergie can't get the ball off me, this time he's playing for the Whites against the Blues in the Nike Family Day at Ibrox

THE HURTING TIME...the tackle that wrecked my career and put me out of football for two-and-a-half years. Take a good look at Simpson's face, you know what he was trying to do

TEARS FOR SOUVENIRS...I can't contain the pain as physio Phil Boersma carries me off. Many criticised him but I SWORE at him and begged to get off that pitch

SCAR ISSUE…the wound from the tackle that launched a thousand stories is on full view as I pound my way back to fitness

DAMAGE ASSESSMENT…in thoughtful mood as I sit it out at pre-season training

SILVER PAIR…seven Finals, seven winner's medals. I love that feeling. Here it's more glory in the Skol Cup in 1992 with Stuart McCall after his goal helped us on the way to a 2-1 win over Aberdeen

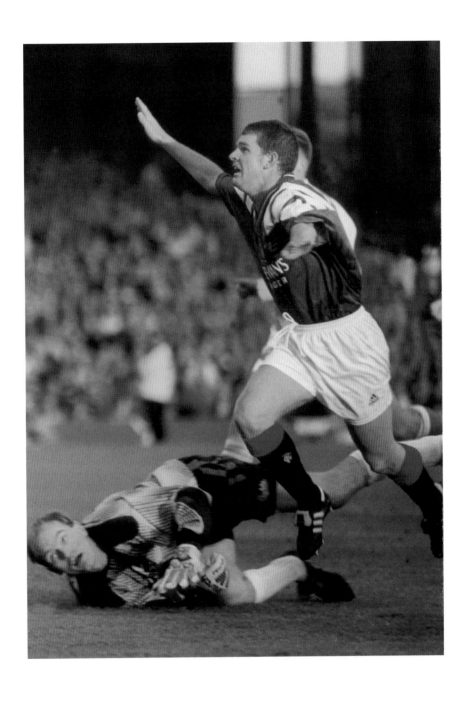

*HIGH AND MIGHTY…eyes up and the ball is on its way
over Jim Leighton to loop in for my goal in the 2-1 League
Cup Final win over Hibs at Parkhead in 1993*

NISSY NICKS MY GLORY…the morning after the night before against Bruges and everyone's buried my goal to talk about big Scott Nisbet's outrageous fluke!

MY LUCKY SHIRT…no not the rather bright Versace number which I wore after the 1-1 draw in Marseille but my prized No.10. Don't know what Coisty's laughing at, look at his waistcoat

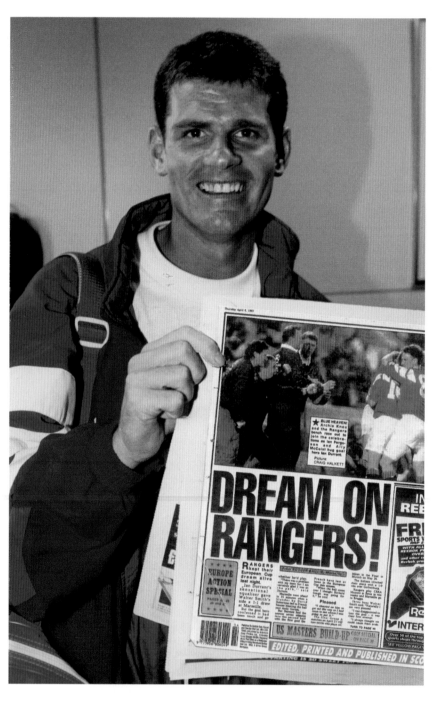

*BACK PAGE NEWS…my goal in the Velodrome against
Marseille means the dream stays alive and I'm in the
limelight. That was the strike of my life*

*GOUGH HIS ROCKER...I lose the plot with skipper
Richard after a goal against - you've guessed it -
Aberdeen. A special moment*

*SUDS YOU LIKE...in the bath with the bubbles and the
League Cup after that memorable win over Hibs in 1993*

THE BLUES BROTHERS…my dream Final. I score, Coisty scores, we win and I get Man of the Match! Victory over the Hibees in 93 was a day to remember

HIDE AND SEEK…playing guess who at a Scotland get together in 1993. I wish I'd been at more

REGRETS I'VE HAD A FEW…and one of them is not playing more alongside a rare talent like Brian Laudrup

TRADING PLACES…for the jersey of Everton, a
worthwhile experience but not a worthwhile manager!

BEST MATCH OF MY LIFE…with Angela on our wedding day. Max and Sophie have simply made what we have always had even stronger

NEW KIT, SAME OLD FACE…in my umpteenth Rangers jersey, the new Nike version. To think I used to wear my brother's cast-offs

*FUTURE'S SO BRIGHT I GOTTA WEAR SHADES…at least
I hope so as I look ahead to life without Rangers*

SECOND CLASS CITIZEN...in action but with no fans behind me, I've had enough of the reserves

PALS FOR LIFE...with the MBE in training, we've been through so much together

SLIMMY DURRANTY...fitness has always meant a lot to me and I have to do more gym work than most because of my knee

BANG ON CUE…with Gordon Durie on tour but he knows I'm unbeatable on my own table at home

*OVER AND OUT...after a creditable Champions League
2-2 draw in Dortmund when Gazza was sent off. I salute
the fans with Durie and Gough*

*JUST GR-EIGHT...It's party time as we celebrate another
title triumph at Ibrox. This time it's number eight*

HISTORY BOOK…with Ally at the launch of Iain King's book to mark nine-in-a-row. I've never been so pleased to see a book come out!

to rap a Keith Wright cross into his own net. Now we needed a rescue act and Walter knew just the man, Ally came on and when you saw him stripped he wasn't his usual slim self. In fact, he was fat.

Yet he scored this incredible bicycle-kick and when he landed the tremors were felt all over Parkhead. No wonder they had to build a new stadium after that.

I always remember how in the shower Ally was going on about how Eusebio was the same with overhead kicks - and he was serious.

No.7 Tennents Scottish Cup Rangers 5 Heart of Midlothian 1
Hampden, May 18, 1996
Scorers: Rangers: Laudrup (2), Durie (3) Hearts: Colquhoun

AGAIN the dilemma Ally and I had come to hate arose. It was me or him, this time for a place on the bench.

Coisty had been struggling with a calf knock but the day before the Final he showed up really well in training and this time the tables were turned on me. He was in and I was out.

I was very down because I'd been confident I would make it and now I was on the outside looking in.

I wished the boys all the best and at about 2.25pm disappeared up the stairs with Charlie Miller to one of the hospitality suites in Hampden to drown my sorrows a little. I soon sank two cans of Boddington's...little realising that a drama had started out on the park.

Coisty had pulled his calf muscle in the warm-up but I was oblivious to this because I was relishing the second can. Then at 2.50pm Jimmy Bell the kitman rushed in and shouted: "Coisty's out, get yerself down the dressing-room."

So I had to nick back to the changing area and sit quietly desperately trying not to breathe on Walter. He's rushing round trying to sort things out and he barks: "OK Durranty, just wait. We need clearance from the ref and Hearts to get you in."

I'm coughing into my sleeve and murmuring: "Fine, Gaffer."

Ref Hugh Dallas came in and OK'd it and then to his eternal credit Hearts boss Jim Jefferies came to comfort Coisty, by now distraught.

Jim said: "Ally, I'm so sorry you're missing the final. Walter, any move you want to make to get someone else in is fine by us. It's no problem."

Coisty wished me all the best through his pain and I was in. I'd had two cans of Boddington's and I was in.

The game, of course, is now a video every Rangers fans should treasure once Brian Laudrup has left the club for Chelsea. He was magnificent that day and - despite Durie's hat-trick - they should call that game the Laudrup Final.

Even without the two goals he scored, one cracking drive into the corner from Durie's lob and one cross that trickled through Gilles Rousset's legs he was immense. He tortured Hearts.

Lauders deserved his celebration afterwards and you knew the club had got to him when he dropped his cosmopolitan cool and you saw him dancing about Hampden wearing a sombrero on the lap of honour.

Then when we got to Ibrox he was on top of the bus with Gazza and the Goalie leading the fans in "Follow, Follow." The man is a hellraiser and I'm concerned he's been a bad influence on the youngsters.

Me? I got on for about 10 minutes and I ran about like a madman. I tried to give my medal to Ally after the game but he wouldn't accept it although I think the Gaffer quietly had one made for him afterwards.

I told Walter later that night how his supersub had played with two cans of Boddington's down his neck and he almost wet himself.

Mind you, if we had lost...

CHAPTER 8

THE GAFFERS

IAN DURRANT has worked with, starred for and tested the patience of four Ibrox legends in the manager's office in his 17 years tied to the club.

From John Greig to Jock Wallace, Graeme Souness to Walter Smith he has seen them scream and lose, smile and win.

Four vastly different characters. From Greig the legendary captain pushed into the manager's office to Wallace the master motivator.

From the simmering genius of Souness to the calm leadership of Smith. Durrant knew them all inside out.

Here he reveals the bust-ups and the big stories that have surrounded the men in charge of Scottish football's biggest club.

THREE weeks before John Greig signed me as a schoolboy, I was already showing I could steal in on the blind side...to nick stray balls from The Albion training ground!

We used to wait until shooting practice on a Friday to blag them but it was a case of needs must as the BB didn't have any and we figured the Gers could afford it.

We were a lively band of kids and I knew every nook and cranny around that training ground. If anyone had come out to chase us they'd never have caught us.

I used to treasure those balls and sometimes when I was kicking one around I'd dream that I was Derek Johnstone or Davie Cooper because I was playing with a football they'd scored with.

Later on in life I'd join in with the likes of DJ and Coop at shooting practice and find they were so good they very rarely missed the target.

So it looks like I was kidding myself - the balls that flew over that fence into my hands probably belonged to Colin Jackson or big Tam Forsyth!

Greig was my first boss at Ibrox but because I was only an apprentice making my way in the game I didn't really spend much time with him.

I was working more with the likes of Stan Anderson and Joe Mason and to be honest I was an awestruck kid in Greig's presence. The only time I really worked with Ledge was on a Friday once I'd broken into the reserves and we would have a mock-up game with the first team.

The big boys hated that because we had a right good team then and would always give them a hard time, often turning them over.

We had Derek and Eric Ferguson, Kenny Black and Billy Davies - all good players. We were a real handful. Those were times when you could watch Greigy enjoying himself before the pressure told.

He came alive on the training field because the truth is he was still a player at heart. He'd been rushed into the manager's chair when big Jock Wallace quit in the wake of his second Treble in three years in 1978.

You only have to look at John's first season to know why being Gers gaffer should carry a government health warning. I mean, he won the League Cup against Aberdeen and then the Scottish Cup 3-2 after extra-time against Hibs in the third match after two 0-0 draws.

Yet people forget that because he committed the ultimate crime in some fans' eyes - his side lost 4-2 to a ten-man Celtic team at Parkhead and surrendered the title.

The hope of back-to-back Trebles was gone and it had all ended in the worst possible fashion.

Winning an Old Firm game is sweet enough, but winning it a man down is the ultimate. I was to taste that twice as a Rangers player - but I'll never forget how bad it felt to experience defeat against ten Celts as a Rangers fan.

On May 21, 1979 I was just a 12-year-old Rangers-daft kid wondering when the next game of football was going to start outside on Craigiehall Street. But I remember everyone ground to a halt, crowding round the tranny to find out what was happening that night at Parkhead.

These days we have wall-to-wall live football coverage from Scotland and England's Premier Leagues, Italy's Serie A and even the Primera Liga in Spain.

Yet that match, an Old Firm title decider, **WASN'T** on the telly. Can you imagine the hype that sort of showdown would attract these days? Richard Keys and Andy Gray would be up here for a week beforehand doing previews.

Celtic needed a win in what was their final match of the season. We could afford to draw and leave ourselves needing just two points from the last two games against Partick Thistle and Hibs.

The game was a 52,000 sell-out and there was little chance of a ticket for me - my mum and dad wouldn't have let me go to an Old Firm game at Parkhead anyway because of the trouble there could be in those days.

So we depended on the radio and you can imagine the reaction when Alex MacDonald - one of Kinning Park's finest - put the Gers ahead after just nine minutes.

They then had Johnny Doyle sent off for kicking wee Doddie and I thought we were on Easy Street, but Roy Aitken and then George McCluskey put them ahead.

Now you were panicking, in a cold sweat, but Bobby Russell - a great favourite of mine - made it 2-2 and soon there were just six minutes left.

We seemed safe. But what happened next was a disaster.

First, big Colin Jackson - the original Bomber before John Brown in the 90s - headed one into his own net before Murdo MacLeod settled it. That was the start of a song that would haunt Rangers fans as much as our Nine-in-a-Row And One To Go has plagued Celtic since we equalled their record.

I can remember the tune to this day. To the tune of Boney M's *Brown Girl in the Ring*, they used to sing: "Ten Men Won The League - Nah,Nah,Nah,Nah,Nah"

You couldn't go near a Celtic fan without hearing it. I hate that song!

My big brother James was a regular then and I can still see him and his pals coming home after that game. I remember looking out the window and seeing them trooping down the road, their scarves hanging off their necks almost apologetically.

They looked like outlaws coming through a deserted town in an old cowboy movie - no one else had gone outside because of the score!

The next morning our *Daily Record* had a picture on the front page of George McCluskey, Davie Provan and big Shuggie Edvaldsson hoisting their skipper Danny McGrain aloft. It sank in then.

Being the manager in charge when something as grave as that happens isn't easily forgiven at Rangers. And I don't know if the fans ever truly forgot it with John.

Greigy went on to have scarce triumphs and a lot of toil, particularly in the league, although he seemed astute in Europe at times.

He was always enthusiastic and I don't think he got the respect he should have had from the older players.

They had been his friends for so long and then he was their boss and they didn't like it. Boards do things like that, promote the skipper to manager and don't think of the consequences.

They do it because they don't know how players think and I really don't think any former player can pull it off.

But Greig was an honest, decent man who'd sweated blood for the club and it's right that he is still a part of it in his PR role nowadays.

Most people credit Jock Wallace with signing me but there's no disputing it was Greigy who first made me put pen to paper on a contract that saw me committed as an S form with an apprenticeship.

And I can even lay claim to playing a part in winning him that tag Ledge. It was early in the Souness era when Graeme thought it would be a good idea to get John out onto the training field with the boys again.

So they hunted him out some boots and gear and there he was rattling around in the seven-a-side game.

Every time he got the ball Coisty and I were shouting: "Here, Gaffer!"

We did it through respect. He'd signed us after all, me as a kid and Coisty at the third attempt from Sunderland for £185,000 in 1983. I still tell Greigy to this day he paid well over the odds!

Still, Souness very quickly had enough of that. I always remember him calling a halt to the game. He picked up the ball like a kid in a street game and pulled me and Ally over to utter the immortal words: "Listen you two, I'M the Gaffer. He's a Legend!".

The name stuck.

I still remember the sadness I felt when John called everyone into the dressing-room and said he was going. For a man who had been with Rangers so long it must have been such a hard thing to do.

He walked out on the biggest job in Scottish football but only he will ever know the toll being the manager of Rangers had taken on him.

I joke with John to this day that if he'd thrown me into the first team at 15 I'd have kept him in a job!

But, seriously, it was a crying shame for Greigy during his reign because he was left to shop in the bargain basement yet he made some superb signings.

He bought players like Robert Prytz and Jim Bett who were way ahead of their time in Scottish football, real quality midfielders.

Prytz played for clubs like Young Boys of Berne, Bayer Uerdingen, Malmo and Verona - he was a Bosman player before they had heard of the Jean-Marc Bosman ruling.

Teams from Switzerland to Germany, Sweden to Italy were just snapping him up for £100,000 every time and he kept moving. But I'll tell you it was shrewd managers that were buying him - he was class.

Yet always John's teams would be say two players short of what he needed and the money was going on rebuilding the stadium. I felt for him and latterly Jock would suffer from the same thing.

But Greigy is a huge man in my eyes. I didn't see as many games of his career at its peak as I'd have liked but the video he made recently is in my collection.

I used to think he was just bragging when he told me about all these wonder goals he used to score. Then I watched the tape and realised he really *is* a legend!

He's a man I'll always respect and that's why I was so shocked recently when he had a heart attack.

I'd been winding him up about something in Ibrox that morning and then a mate phoned an hour later to say he'd been rushed to hospital, his recovery meant the world to me.

In the last three years I've lost two of my biggest influences at Rangers in Davie Cooper and Big Jock and I'm not ready to lose another. Wallace was something else, a ferocious Rangers fan who became the manager.

Every time I see Andy Gray on Sky Sports displaying the tactics with those draughts I think of the big man. Jock used to do the same on a Friday and before an Old Firm game the draughts would be flying all over the bloody place!

Jock loved back-to-front football, the midfield got missed out and you were expected to get there and back up the likes of Derek Johnstone or Coisty. Jock was in his second spell, of course, but the principles were the same. He was a war-time jungle-fighter and I'll tell you what you knew it in his team-talks. They were classics.

He'd be saying: "We're in the trenches, lads, that's where we are.

"Now get over the top, fix your bayonets and stick it right intae them!"

I'd pipe up: "But boss, it's **FOOTBALL** we're playing."

And he'd give me a clout round the ear and reply: "Shut it, Durranty, you know what ah ******* mean."

What a motivator he was. You'd be sitting there nervous before an Old Firm game and all of a sudden the silence would be shattered by Jock leading a chorus of "Follow, Follow."

His assistant Alex Totten has a love of the game I've never seen beaten and I loved his training. Nothing was done without the ball.

I lapped that up because so often Jock had us throwing up doing the physical stuff on Gullane Sands. But those Trebles in 1976 and 1978 and what he did for Gers earned him the place he deserves in history.

He's probably up in heaven right now, telling some midfielder to get his lazy arse up that cloud!

When Jock went we got Souness and by now although I was only 19 I'd played around 50 league games and considered myself established.

That makes a difference. Now I needed an influence and I got it in a guy who for me was on a pedestal as a player. He came in with the perfect backing in Walter Smith, they had the ideal blend.

Everything changed when Souness arrived and I mean everything. From flip-flops in the shower to the compulsory eating of pasta.

Nowadays, I eat pasta as second nature. We had many a lunch in a Italian restaurant in Glasgow called Sarti's talking over the old times to complete this book.

But back then I hated pasta - the closest I got to cultured eating was going to the China Sea for a businessman's lunch. Chicken and mushroom soup followed by steak and chips for a fiver, thanks very much!

I learned a lot about football from Souness, too. People say the runs I make can't be coached but I'd counter that by saying I only began to make them because I played with a genius in Davie Cooper.

I knew he couldn't beat absolutely everyone on the other team - he only did that sometimes. So I'd get beyond him and he'd hit me with these slide-rule passes.

But when the streetwise Souness came there were other things to learn, he taught me so much about the art of keeping possession. He'd been bred on it at Liverpool and honed it in Italy with Sampdoria. He'd reason with me saying: "Durranty, what can they do to you if they don't have the ball?"

We'd play games on smaller pitches, we'd play three against six where you had to work so hard to keep the ball. It made us better players.

I was raw, I was young and he was putting good habits into me. I used to actually count the times I gave the ball away in games and if was four times then Souness made me want it to be twice next time.

That was Souness the manager but what about Souness the man? Well, that was the cause of a thousand arguments between me and Ally.

Now I'd start this by saying I would **ALWAYS** have Coisty in my team but they just never saw eye to eye. Me? I loved Souness, I thought he was excellent.

But Graeme and Ally just never clicked and that should be something they both regret these days. There's no doubt in my mind it was a personality clash.

Ally was the King of Ibrox when Souness arrived and there was a point to be made. Only one man could be the King and that was Graeme.

90

He quickly brought in Mark Hateley and Mo Johnston and Ally went through what was his most difficult spell with the club. Any time he played he would do Souness a turn but the next week the teamsheet would go up and The Judge was still on the bench.

Ally was in the doldrums when Mark was struggling in his first season in 90-91 and Souness was still persevering with him. You have to say that Mark went on to do great things but there's an unwritten rule that players judge managers by.

If the guy in your position isn't doing it then you deserve at least one chance to show you are better. Coisty never really got that from Graeme.

He was to prove him wrong with two Golden Boots and I have to say that my favourite Gers striking partnership was Mo and Ally and NOT Hateley and McCoist. I thought Coisty and Johnston were a bigger goal threat.

But Souness loved target men and let's face it Hateley was one helluva player. But I've always regretted Graeme's feuds with McCoist.

He was constantly at war too with the SFA and they'd call him to Park Gardens like some schoolboy who'd been out of order.

But he was never fazed by the things that happened because always there at the core of him was this belief that he was the best, his team was the best. Well, we started to believe him.

I remember the bad times like when Ally went to Cheltenham races on his day off and was fined and I'd think the Gaffer was out of order but I knew he'd never change his mind. My only disagreement with him was that I wanted McCoist in the team.

Ally showed his strength of character too then, though, because everyone and their Auntie was saying he should walk away.

That's an easy thing to say if you're not at Rangers. What if you're there and you're looking at the calibre of players being signed and you want to be part of it all?

No Coisty did the right thing, one sticky patch wouldn't have justified leaving a top club where he was to rule the roost for the best part of 14 years.

I used to give him comfort and advice and then eventually I just gave him abuse. He was calling me Graeme's right-hand man!

I just said: "The Gaffer's right, you really are crap!"

Seriously, Souness was hard on Ally and although they laugh about it now, that was the classic case of two big egos, two stubborn men against each other and only ONE winner. It's a shame because it didn't need to be like that.

It got to the stage where Ally came off the bench and scored two belters against Aberdeen and Souness didn't even clap!

Graeme was a deep man, a very complex person and I don't think I ever got near him. It takes a special person to know him and I didn't do it, but we have a nice relationship where I know that at any time in my life we will be able to sit and have a laugh and a beer.

I'm happy with that.

Souness was such a success at Rangers because of one man - the Great Waldo. That's what Coisty and I call Mr Smith, especially when we're begging for a game every week!

The man has been a breath of fresh air to both of us because he knows we like a laugh and he knows we love Rangers.

And I also feel he knows when we leave Ibrox a little bit of the heart will be ripped out of the place and I'm not being big-headed saying that.

I've spoken earlier about the hurt when I was dropped for the Nine-in-a-Row game at Tannadice but that doesn't mean I'm bitter or that I'd stick the knife in Walter's back.

I feel we are both Rangers men who would put the club first and I have so much respect for him. The stress levels have gone up for Walter these last few years, I have no doubt about that.

He is a Rangers fan trying his utmost to win trophies for the club and I have seen changes in him, seen him doing things he wouldn't have done a few years ago when he was more laid-back. That's pressure. He's desperate to go out a winner.

All through the 12 years at Rangers, though, Walter has had his mean streak as well as his dignity.

I remember one day when I was having a nightmare and when I'm nervous or under pressure I laugh. I've been like that all my life.

Well, I did it one day when he was slaughtering me and before I knew it he had me by the throat pinned against the wall. I stopped laughing.

Then in the 1991 Skol Cup semi against Hibs, which we eventually lost 1-0 to Keith Wright's header, he'd been giving me the warning to stay wide right - a position I really do hate.

I kept drifting inside, we were losing and he was livid. At half-time he kicked a hamper full of boots about six feet across the floor and he must have hurt himself.

I couldn't snigger then, though - I went white thinking: "That hamper could have been my balls!"

What I know for sure is that Rangers would never have won Nine-in-a-Row without Walter Smith. He's been criticised about Europe but there are so many difficulties there, playing so early in the season and trying to get all the new signings to gel.

The level of stick has been high for Walter and people accuse our fans of being spoiled by success but they only enjoy winning as much as the players. Who wants to be a loser?

Hard fact is that while Rangers have no divine right to win anything the amount of money being spent on players means they should be in for every trophy they contest. That requires a special manager and for the last seven years we've had one.

Now he's going and I for one think it's too early. Yet he's sacrificed his family growing up for Rangers and maybe he's right to think of himself now. Maybe this is the time to recharge his batteries, the time in his life to get ready for the next challenge.

But I feel he's only 50 and too young to quit and move "upstairs" at Gers for long, he's too good a manager and he'd prove that in the English Premiership.

Whatever happens he's off and he'll miss McCoist and Durrant - his comedians, the men who keep morale going and the welcoming committee for foreigners.

For instance, our young Finnish winger Jonatan Johansson survived his first Christmas in Scotland in the Durrant household.

But like all my bosses now I've done my bit for Rangers, played my games, won some medals and had some laughs. It's time to move on.

CHAPTER 9

IBROX INSIDER

HE has been the beating heart of the Ibrox dressing-room and no-one knows the Rangers stars better than Ian Durrant.

But behind the public image, what are the heroes who make the headlines really like?

Here joker-in-the-pack Durranty explodes some myths and remembers the legends of an emotional Rangers past that will be swept away in the new Dick Advocaat era.

Ian has been at the centre of a hundred pranks. The laughs will stay with him wherever his career leads him next.

Yet there has also been a time for grieving, when he lost a man he'd come to regard as family.

I'VE made so many friends in a lifetime at Rangers, but never one to replace the man I lost. Davie Cooper.

It's three years now since the day Coop was snatched away from us and there are still times when I reach for the 'phone to call him. There's still a part of me that doesn't believe he's gone, a part of me that doesn't want to believe we lost him at the age of just 39.

March 22 will never be a happy anniversary in the Durrant household but just a day I sit down and remember the loss of a great player and a true friend.

I'll never forget the numb feeling that washed over me when Coisty came on the phone that awful day and said Coop had taken a brain haemorrhage while he was coaching kids for a TV show at Broadwood.

Coisty was falling to pieces but he managed to explain that he was going up to the hospital with Derek Johnstone and I should stay in touch. All I was thinking was "Please Coop, please Coop. Pull through."

I prayed he'd recover and went into the park the next day but Davie Dodds walked into the dressing-room and said training had been cancelled because Coop was dead.

Some people shuffled off to the gym or somewhere quiet but I just put my things on and came back home to be with Angela. I couldn't believe it then and I still don't now.

I was totally devastated. After all, I had been with him at the races the week before and he was full of life. Ally and I helped each other through it but it was harder for his brother John and his mum and dad.

You could see by the turnout at the funeral how much people appreciated him. Celtic fans came and hung their scarves on the gates of Ibrox and that says it all.

Coisty hadn't slept. He'd been at the hospital when Coop arrived and then he was a pall-bearer. It hit him so hard and the loss will always live with both of us.

There's a Davie Cooper suite at Ibrox now and it's beautiful, a fitting tribute. I've gone in there at quiet times and just remembered him because he was such a gem of a fella. That isn't a tear-stained tribute. I'd tell him the same if he was alive today - and God, how I wish he was.

The public at large was only just getting to know the real Coop through his TV and media work.

He'd been stung early on in his career by criticism from the Press and he decided there and then not to speak to them. That gave him this moody blue tag but it was miles off the mark.

He was such a funny man whose one-liners could slay you. Yet I always remember him as the victim of a belter one day at Hamilton races. Coisty said: "There's a horse in the 3.40 and it's a cert but bloody Hell I just can't remember the name. Hey, Coop what is it? I can't remember it but I can tell you it begins with A, though."

Coop is pleading for the name by now, sniffing out a win. And he's roaring through the form card desperate to come up with this horse.

He sees one and bellows out "Amnesia!"

Coisty grins: "That's it! that's the one I couldn't remember."

Done up like a kipper - but at least Coop saw the funny side.

As a footballer I used to know when he was going to have a genius Saturday. We used to have Scotland-England games at training on a Friday and he would take the utter mickey out of the great Terry Butcher. That's when you knew he was up for the game the next day.

I remember so many great games from him. I watched in awe one night as he bamboozled Finnish team Ilves Tampere all on his own. I've never seen so many nutmegs!

The fans would gasp, but I expected it of Davie because I knew he was The Master. We played Aberdeen in that memorable 3-3 Skol Cup Final draw in 1987 - which we eventually won with my clinching penalty in the shoot-out - and we got a free-kick.

I fancied myself as a bit of a David Beckham in those days and I was going to take it when Coop pushed me out of the way.

He said to me: "Leighton won't even see this."

Then he rocketed an unbelievable goal into the top corner and as fate would have it we met up with Scotland a week later.

Jim comes over and says to Coop: "You know Davie, I almost got my fingertips to that ball."

Davie, deadpan as ever, replied: "Aye, on the way back out."

I couldn't stop laughing, but I was flabbergasted that he could say something like that to someone like Jim Leighton.

Coop was a one-off whose memory still makes me laugh before the sadness kicks in again. If he was helping me go down Memory Lane he'd have wanted my Rangers pals down the years to be ridiculed and embarrassed so here goes:

ALLY McCOIST: Everyone knows the laughs and the jokes we have had together at Rangers, some of the stories have gone into legend.

But the part the fans don't see is the deep friendship we have away from the Cup finals and the nights out. We have been through some very difficult times together.

We were both very close to our dads and when they died we were there to support each other. We have such a close bond.

Being a footballer is the sort of occupation where you make passing acquaintances because players will move on and you lose touch.

That will never be the case with Ally and I. We will be friends until the day we die.

He introduces me to people as the wee brother he never had and I've always looked up to him, though not too much!

Everyone sees the happy-go-lucky Coisty who is always on top of the world. Golden Bollocks or simply a lucky bastard as the Gaffer famously christened him.

But I've been through the tough times with him too, through the death of his dad, through the broken leg and through the fights with Souness. Ally's an emotional person and he's had his share of tears.

But it's a testament to his character the way he has come back. How many times have you seen Coisty written off?

But he's still here battling to keep playing and juggle that with being a chat-show host with an MBE.

Yet he's not always the smiler the cameras love. I'll tell you what he can be a torn-faced git too. Don't go near McCoist when he's in one of his moods.

We've had some great fall-outs on the training ground when we've been having howlers and when you're toiling one stray word can spark it all off.

We've been separated a few times but never actually got a punch in yet which is fine by me, I don't fancy my chances!

Our arguments are generally over his shocking first touch. I'll be screaming: "Coisty, you're 35, you've lost it and the Queen Mary turns quicker." He hates digs about his age.

Yet if we do have a bust-up it's sorted by the time we get back to the dressing-room and we're laughing at each other.

I've loved playing beside him and I've got so many great memories of his goals but one sticks in my mind, more for his stupid celebration.

It was in that incredible 4-4 draw with Celtic in 1986 when he smashed one low into the corner from 25 yards and hared off to the touchline. He stood there with no emotion on his face then kissed his hand and whacked his right boot. Ludicrous.

One other occasion that sticks with me because it meant so much to him was his goals in the Champions League when we beat Grasshopper of Zurich 2-1.

For years I'd slaughtered him about his duck amongst Europe's elite and then finally he got two. He took his shirt off and waved it above his head to celebrate and earn a booking but he didn't care.

He'd done that to taunt me and he was howling up at the stand: "How do you like that, would you like a slice of me now?" Nutter.

He has broken almost every record in the book now apart from beating my Scottish Cup medals. I've got three and he's got one which is sad because I can also point to my two Man of the Match awards from those Finals. He detests that.

You've got to laugh with Ally, though, if you can't you've got no sense of humour.

I remember back in the early days he did this modelling shoot and he was dressed up in a black leather suit with one of those caps trying to look like a butch American cop. Instead he looked gay and like that guy out of The Village People!

I was in stitches and I got hold of a copy of the picture to bring in and pin up all over Ibrox. That's where the McCoist cunning came in.

He drove down to my mum's and said: "Alright if I come in a minute Ruby I just want to see your photo album of the wee man's goals."

He's busy telling my mum what a great player I am while stealing this YMCA photo out of the book and ripping it up. What a ponce!

PAUL GASCOIGNE: A bundle of joy to be with but he goes at 100mph for 24 hours a day. We're talking about a guy who needs one hour kip and then he's recharged.

He is the most generous person I have seen in my life. He gives tramps every penny in his pocket and gets the bus home on a night out. That's the type of fella he is.

Okay, he has a lot of money but so do plenty of other people and they don't walk up to kids on the street and give them a fiver.

This reputation as a boozer bewilders me because he can't drink. He's very bad at it. Try taking him to TGI Fridays for cocktails and you're on a winner. It's a cheap night.

Angela and I have had Paul out to stay with us and he's spent hours in my pool room trying to beat me on my own table which is impossible. If he plays any sport he simply must win, from tennis to ping pong.

His life is bizarre. His level of fame is up there with someone like Madonna. I've had people moan at me, saying going out with me is hard because every 20 seconds someone will come up and talk to you or ask for your autograph.

Well, believe me, I've been out with Gazza and it's every two seconds with him. He gets no peace and people then constantly want to paint him as a bad boy which makes players like myself who are close to him so angry.

Everyone wants to slaughter Paul but the Rangers players feel very protective towards him because we are the ones who see the REAL Gazza and I, for one, like what I see.

What you have is a lad who is almost like a kid all the time, as far as I'm concerned he doesn't have a bad bone in his body.

Everyone knows about Gazza the footballer. He's brilliant and temperamental. Story over.

So now they need to know more, they need to know about his wife and his wee boy, his marital problems and the next thing. Where does it stop, the man has been hounded for three years in Scotland.

The English tabloid papers are the ones who created Gazza in the first place and now they are the ones who have made his life a misery. We've played pool at my house and he enjoys being in the back room having a laugh away from it all.

He'll tell me then that he is actually SCARED to come out of his house at night because of the constant attention. That can't be right.

Here's an example. We went for a meal together once and there were six photographers camped outside the restaurant.

When we'd finished the reporters with them were in asking what we'd drank, eaten, the whole nine yards. When I read the stories next day the two bottles of red we'd had became six and I had a taste of life as Gazza.

I thought then that when incidents like that happen it's no wonder he sometimes comes across as paranoid.

He's a person who takes those personal things that have happened in his life badly but he didn't bring it into the dressing-room.

His departure to Middlesbrough was the end of a spell where I believe he truly found happiness for the first time since his Newcastle days.

Rangers have been good for him but football is a massive business now and that dictated that he moved on. I'll miss him.

He's the most famous player in Britain and the BEST player in Britain. I realise the English media want to put him down for playing in what they see as a weak league these past three years. Well they have him back now and they should treat him right.

If they want to win France 98 they will have to rely on one person and one person only. And we put him together again at Rangers.

The one, the only. Gazza.

DEREK JOHNSTONE: My first room partner on my first Rangers trip, to Chelsea to play in a game to raise money for the victims of the Bradford City fire disaster.

I was to score my first Gers goal - a penalty as we lost 3-2 - but before the game I had to put up with his incessant farting. I wasn't brave enough to tell him, I just shut up and made him his tea in the morning.

But apart from his obvious drawbacks, DJ is a good man who has always stood by me. He works for Radio Clyde as a football reporter now and I think he comes across as not too biased!

TERRY BUTCHER: I could go on all day about his playing qualities but the fans perhaps didn't see that behind the scenes he was the complete captain.

He was the one who would deal with the Press, the bonuses, the players to go to Player of the Year dances.

Even when he was injured he saw all that as part of his job and happily did it. He was simply delighted to be called the skipper of Rangers. A proud man and the way he left after a bust-up with Graeme Souness was shabby.

JIMMY NICHOLL: He has a love and an enthusiasm for football that are unparalleled by any coach I know. I worked with him a few times in the reserves when he wasn't playing and everything was geared to getting the ball down on the deck and playing. It hasn't surprised me he's highly rated as a manager.

GRAHAM ROBERTS: Conducting the fans singing The Sash in that infamous 2-2 game with Celtic in 1987 made him a legend and he had an incredible impact on the club in two short years.

The 1998 version of Robbo is Rino Gattuso who has won his way into the fans' hearts with his 100 per cent and the rest attitude.

It was a shame that Graham ended up playing for the thirds in Mallaig and places like that after he fell out with Souness.

Things could have been settled a lot better than that and if there was one thing that left a bitter taste in my mouth about Souness it was the way Terry and Graham left the club.

Yet you can see by the reception they both get any time they're at Ibrox that the fans know they gave their heart and soul to the club.

ANDY GORAM: If Rangers find a better keeper then he will have to be a ROBOT.

He's unique because if he trains really hard one day he's too stiff in the joints to do much the next. Sure, there are keepers who work harder.

But all that matters at a football club is what you do on matchday and he's the best.

Andy knows his own preparation and it works for him. And off the field he's great company. He's a fish fanatic and he has been known occasionally to follow that with one or two glasses of claret.

He introduced me to clam chowder and all that stuff on holiday once and his diet is actually quite healthy for a Flying Hippo.

I'll concede that this is not a man who looks like an athlete. He has teeth like condemned buildings because he is terrified of the dentist. I hope he gets them fixed because he's running out of teeth and I can't keep looking at those stumps after his crowns have been knocked out.

JOHN BROWN: He does this trick with Drambuie where you light the drink, stick your hand over the glass, then suck in the fumes. I'll never forget Nigel Spackman trying it, missing and ending up with sticky liqueur all over his head on his first day out with the Gers players.

There's Hannibal Lecter over him grinning: "See youse English yese cannae handle it."

He's mad the Bomber. I remember Ally had this great idea once of taking John and I to see his favourite band Stiff Little Fingers. It seemed a good shout until we remembered it was St Patrick's Day and we were the only Rangers fans in the place.

Ally knows the SLF singer Jake Burns and we had really good tickets sitting near the lighting deck which I thought was great because we could hide there and watch the show. Not Bomber he's leaping up and down, dancing and shouting until all the Celtic fans in the crowd finally turn round and see who we are.

We got pelters that night and I was glad to make a sharp exit!

On a serious note, Bomber's young daughter Lauren had a heart defect and the people at Yorkhill Sick Children's Hospital, who I admire so much, looked after her royally.

Bomber's never forgotten that and he's a kind of balding Jimmy Saville, doing bike rides and everything for their funds. That's John.

If you wanted one person to have the pleasure of scoring against Celtic for Rangers it was Bomber and he did it in a 3-1 win at Parkhead. His celebrations seemed to last about three days.

I hope Dick Advocaat keeps him around as a coach at Rangers because you need someone to remind people of the roots of the club.

TERRY HURLOCK: A typical Cockney, he was a very hard player who rivalled even Souness. Off the pitch he had all this knocked-off gear from tracksuits to these belting Persian rugs. Christ knows where he got them.

IAN FERGUSON: He has played from the heart since the day he signed and he could well be the last player to get a testimonial from Rangers Football Club. He's earned it.

He has always been a good friend and he's the sort of player who is called in after two months out and plays superbly.

Don't forget that ten years ago he was a £1m player. He was ahead of his time.

A tee-totaller who comes on every night out so he can tell us all what we did the next morning! Has the occasional Rolling Rock and if he does stay out of his way.

BRIAN LAUDRUP: His life revolves around his family and he handles it right by keeping them out of the limelight. A happy house means a happy player and he knows that.

I feel he was stabbed in the back by a few people in the run-up to the move to Chelsea and it upset him that the fans found out the way they did.

Brian takes things like that to heart because he is a sincere person. He has taken me aside a few times since he came and said he can't believe I'm not in this squad or that squad. They may only have been words of comfort but from a player of his stature they have always perked me up.

He's a wine connoisseur and any time we go to a fancy restaurant we take the menu off Lauders and give him the wine list to do the choosing.

Rates alongside Coop as the most graceful player I've seen in Light Blue although I'm sure he won't slaughter me for giving Davie the edge.

The 5-1 Scottish Cup Final over Hearts in 1996 should always be remembered as his Final.

RICHARD GOUGH: If there is a player any player should want to come back as in his next life it's Goughie. He is the ultimate professional.

His matchday preparation and organisation are second to none. I've never known anyone so methodical with his approach to his fitness.

If you go to a Rangers game, watch him at the warm-up. He's already gone through a complex set of stretches in the dressing-room, remember.

And while others are kicking balls around or doing their own little thing he has a specially devised routine that takes him through running, passing and heading before the first whistle has blown. It can be minus two or eighty degrees and he'll never change it.

I enjoy my gym work a lot but Goughie rivals me. They've called Richard and I The Thoroughbreds over the years and he's earned the tag.

STUART McCALL: He's a human dynamo and the only ginger-haired guy I'd pick for my team because I always end up fighting with them! Seriously, if I was a boss he'd be my first pick.

His tombstone will say Bradford City, Everton, Rangers and Scotland - killed by a groundsman for unnecessary slide-tackling!

When Stuart dies there will be a big furrow of turf as he slides his way into the grave with his studs up.

He rooms now with the Rocket Man, GORDON DURIE, whose workrate is incredible on a park these days for someone of his age. He should finish his career at Ibrox because he has done a superb job for the team.

CHARLIE MILLER: Part of the Spice Boys with Derek McInnes and a kid who has the ability to be a great with Rangers and Scotland.

Known as Spud - he's from Castlemilk and he'd have chips with his pasta - all he needs to do is screw the head and it's all there for him.

He will always be a good player but he could be a genius. I can see it in him because he reminds me of myself at that age.

I know the pitfalls on and off the park and I've tried to knock sense into him but it's a hard job. He has this winning little smile and he'll slag my ears and call me "Lugs Bunny" and the lesson is lost. But I'm sure he's listening.

CRAIG MOORE: I was an usher at his wedding and he's become a very close friend since he moved in near to my home in Bothwell.

Mooro or Mince Man because I'm convinced he fell into a pot of the stuff soon after his birth in Australia. How else do you explain all those freckles?

Seriously, if he plays in the centre of defence - his true position - then he can be the next Richard Gough. That's how highly I rate him.

DEREK McINNES: The vainest man in the world, he has even made a formal complaint to Walter Smith that there aren't enough mirrors in the dressing-room!

He was furious when LORENZO AMORUSO was signed because he's better-looking and his tan is real.

He was originally signed to make the team photo look better but now he has a new two-year deal and that will be his proving time because he's a smashing player. That will be £20 please, Del.

MARCO NEGRI: Allegedly , the new Moody Blue but he's actually a very funny lad. The new Coisty is how you should describe him.

If he hadn't had his eye injury in this his first season you would have been looking at 60 goals. His main dream is to make Italy's World Cup squad and considering he's the top-scoring Italian in the world I don't understand why he's not there.

They may look upon it as an inferior league too but he would score in any company. I've enjoyed watching him this season and the Italians are nice people.

SERGIO PORRINI is a gentleman and RINO GATTUSO is loved by the fans already because of that all-action style.

Marco and Co. will be around at a club that I won't be part of but I hope players like Ally and I have taught them something about the real Rangers.

The secret has been to play together, sulk together, win together, smile together. Always together - that's Rangers.

CHAPTER 10

FIRM FAVOURITE

FEW players know the emotion and the intensity of the Old Firm clash better than Ian Durrant.

From the moment he scored on his derby debut against Celtic he was established as the star all Light Blues fans wanted to see in against their bitterest rivals.

So often in their hour of need the man who has popped up with the goal to silence the Celts has been Durrant.

He relishes every Old Firm win to the limit and goes into hiding when he loses to the Hoops. This is the player who doesn't need to kiss the badge on his jersey to show he loves his club.

Now after 13 years playing in the heart of the Glasgow conflict he can look back on a football life spent feuding in the greatest club game of them all.

THERE is no other game like it, no other game that has such power that peoples' lives revolve around it. That's the Old Firm.

Listen, whatever some may think I'm not a bigot. But I don't care who knows it, Rangers v Celtic is a match that means the world to me.

I grew up in Kinning Park, bred on tales of great clashes between football's bitterest rivals and I'm one of the lucky ones to have played in it.

We are talking here about a game that can mean two months of heartache if you lose and a constant yearning for revenge. This is NOT a normal game of football.

You just have to win. Simple as that.

On the occasions I have lost to Celtic it's hard to describe how it feels. You're desolate.

And I have to admit sportsmanship is last on my agenda just then. I'm always first off the park, you don't want to hang around out there.

I have gone off when we've lost and shaken hands with no-one. Losing hurts too much. If they'd won I would at times seek out Peter Grant because we became friends through our fights on the pitch but that's about as far as it went.

I believe Peter is a true Celtic man who loves the club and respects its traditions. He may be at Norwich City but you know where his heart is. Wherever I go it will be the same when I leave Rangers.

We recognised that in ourselves and in some ways our careers have been mirror images. We were Scotland under-18s and 21s together, but sadly never the full team because he had even fewer caps than me!

I would count Peter as a close friend now. He moved close to my house near the end of his Celtic stay and we'd go for a couple of beers in the Bothwell Bridge Hotel together.

So, yes, if we lost I would look for Granty but really when Celtic have won it is their moment and for me there is a code, a way to behave.

One of the few times I've seen it broken was that Celtic huddle after the 2-0 Cup win in our nine-in-a-row season. That stuck in my throat and as I've said, as a Glasgow boy I always remembered it.

I'll say it again - foreigners who have come to either club can't believe what they're involved in. They read things and they think they've seen it and done it and that they'll adapt.

And after 10 minutes they don't know WHERE they are.

Even Brian Laudrup's first Celtic game bypassed him and we lost 2-0 but he's more than made up for it since.

Scottish players know more of what's expected and however the Old Firm develop in the future under Dick Advocaat and Wim Jansen they will always have a nucleus of Scots because of that.

It's a fixture that has taken me through the mill since I first faced Celtic's top team in 1985. From the cheers when you win to the tears when the unthinkable happens. Even when I was injured I couldn't get enough of it. I still went to all the games against the Hoops on the District Bar double-decker, although not on the top floor with the madmen. I'm respectable now!

I'd be downstairs with my pal Davie Currie who owns the District and my brother Alan and upstairs you'd have characters like Alan Britton.

For me Brittsy - or Harry the Hedgehog as we called him after some shocking haircuts - sums up what it's like to be a Rangers diehard. He goes everywhere and if he doesn't have a ticket he's a bag of nerves.

I can't bear to see him like that and usually look after him. I mean, we are talking about a guy here who before that famous league decider with Aberdeen in 1991 was up pacing the streets at six in the morning!

With fans like that behind you those were memorable days because at that time you had 17,000 supporters in the Rangers end at Parkhead whereas these days it's half that. It was an amazing atmosphere then.

I remember going to one Old Firm game with the injured John Brown and his pals in a mini-bus that held 12 and there were 25 of us in there for the trip from Blantyre.

The Ibrox insurance man would have loved that!

But for me going to support the team was second nature. Yet it would astound people to know that as a kid Celtic were sniffing around me. It would have been very hard if they were the only team in for me. My heart lies at Ibrox.

Who knows what I would have done had they been the only team interested? Luckily, the likes of Jack Steedman at Clydebank, Queen's Park Rangers, Wolves and Barnsley all wanted me.

As soon as I knew Rangers were in, though, there was no debate. I was to be involved in enough derby drama to fill a book never mind a chapter - and it all started on the day I scored on my Old Firm debut...

DATELINE: Premier League: Ibrox, November 9, 1985:
Rangers 3 Celtic 0

THERE are dreams for every kid as he grows up loving football. To score the winner for Scotland against England, to score the clincher in the World Cup Final.

For me the fantasy was always in my head, scoring for Rangers against Celtic at Ibrox. Within 30 minutes of my Old Firm bow it came true. The goal was a stramash but even now I remember every split-second.

I made a run near post and got a flick on a cross but there was a block and then when I turned round Pat Bonner was lying to the left of the net - the ball was in front of me and the goal was gaping!

I turned round and toe-poked it home, the ball scuttled in and didn't

106

even hit the back of the net. Unbelievable. That day was to be the first of so many duels against Paul McStay and Peter Grant and I should have been frozen with nerves. When you're 18 you're too stupid to think about that, though, so I just fired in.

If ever there was a day Derek Ferguson and I came of age that was it. Despite their experience and the boost they had taken from signing striker Mark McGhee from SV Hamburg and handing him his debut against us it was the two teenagers who were thriving.

Fergie was out of this world for the first-half hour until he was crocked in a challenge with Paul McGugan. Even without him we pulverised them. That set me off in Old Firm games and I have had a great record since. I'll never forget the first goal against them, though.

I was still staying at my mum's and I got the freedom of Kinning Park that night. I went out with my brother but I was beyond celebrating, I was shattered.

That day had started with me certain I'd be **DROPPED** because I felt the Gaffer would change the team and go for experience. There were a few butterflies when big Jock Wallace eventually named the team.

However, he had the guts to stick with Derek and I and we repaid him.

What a midfield that was. Myself and Del in the middle, Coop wide on the left and Ted McMinn wide on the right.

Everyone knows my regard for Coop - and Ted? Well, Ted was a little bit...er...*different* because even Ted didn't know what Ted was doing with the ball! What chance did anyone else have?

Coisty used to pull his hair out because he'd make this great run and McMinn would check back to run out and beat the corner-flag again.

You're talking about a guy who kicked the flag taking a corner at Dumbarton then scored **DIRECT** from one in the same game!

Another day against Clydebank he went on the best mazy run I have ever seen. He beat seven players and drew his foot back to smack it in before taking the most enormous divot you've ever seen and crumpling to the turf. He got up and was given a standing ovation!

He never knew if it was New Year or New York but I remember him giving Derek Whyte water on the head trying to mark him one day and that summed up his ability.

He wasn't superstar material, Ted, but he had this great affinity with the Rangers fans because they will always love a character.

RANGERS: Walker, Dawson, McPherson, McKinnon, Munro, D. Ferguson, Bell, Durrant, McCoist, Williamson, Cooper. Subs: Russell, McMinn.

CELTIC: Bonner, W. McStay, McAdam, Aitken, McGugan, Burns, Provan, MacLeod, Grant, McGhee, McClair. Subs: McGrain, Johnston.

DATELINE: Premier League: Ibrox, March 22, 1986:
Rangers 4 Celtic 4

THERE have been some incredible games against Celtic, none more so than this.

We were down and out at 3-1 and then they had Willie McStay sent off and we annihilated them for 25 mad minutes.

Cammy Fraser scored twice and Robert Fleck got the luck of an incredible deflection.

The wind-ups on the park that day were legendary at times and big Roy Aitken was at the middle of it with McCoist. After Murdo MacLeod's eventual equaliser tied it all up Roy was hunting for Ally to slag him and Coisty - who'd scored his usual goal earlier - flipped his jersey over his head to hide!

My sparring partner was always, of course, Peter Grant. We were never out of each other's faces spitting venom. We were two men on opposite sides of the fence, two men who both love their clubs.

But in the end there was just one word that would tell you about our relationship. Respect.

RANGERS: Walker, Burns, Munro, McPherson, McKinnon, Durrant, I. Ferguson, Russell, McCoist, Fleck, McMinn. Subs: Cooper, D. Ferguson.

CELTIC: Bonner, W. McStay, Whyte, Aitken, O'Leary, MacLeod, McClair, P. McStay, Johnston, Burns, Archdeacon. Subs: Grant, McInally.

DATELINE: Premier League: Ibrox, August 31, 1986:
Rangers 1 Celtic 0

THIS was the first ever live televised league game on a Sunday and that brought a pressure of its own on a day when we knew they'd have opened up a gap and turned the critics on the Souness Revolution.

My worries beforehand were unfounded as I actually scored twice - one was disallowed. An offside decision I swear to this day was a crime.

The pass Davie Cooper gave me for the goal that did count was quite simply the best pass I have ever seen in my life. He took FOUR players out with one reverse ball.

Coop wasn't even looking at me, he simply knew I was coming.

He slipped it and I ran into oceans of space to guide it low past Pat Bonner.

The sad thing for Davie is that he stood waiting to catch me in the celebrations and I gave him a custard pie in the face and ran right past him!

I just couldn't wait to get to the Enclosure to join in the fun and Jimmy Nicholl and Cammy Fraser eventually caught me.

Yep, scoring in the Rangers-Celtic game is a dream and I've been lucky enough to live that out - more than once!

Of the five goals I've scored against Celtic - and I still maintain Laudrup stole the sixth with that nine-in-a-row strike - this was my favourite.

And the great thing was it filled some pockets in the District Bar too because when I got the nod I was playing I would always phone them and let them know.

Right away the wedge went on Durrant for first goal and I usually came in at around 12-1. Come to think of it I never have seen any of their winnings.

RANGERS: Woods, Nicholl, Munro, D. Ferguson, McPherson, Butcher, Fraser, McMinn, McCoist, Durrant, Cooper. Subs: Nisbet, Fleck.

CELTIC: Bonner, Grant, Whyte, Aitken, McGugan, MacLeod, McClair, P. McStay, Johnston, Burns, Archdeacon. Subs: McInally, W. McStay.

DATELINE: Skol Cup Final: Hampden, October 26, 1986:
Rangers 2 Celtic 1

THE league result was still fresh in our minds before this showdown and I have to tell you the patter on the park was flying.

I blasted one home from close range after getting a lucky break from a Cammy Fraser free-kick and that wasn't his only contribution.

Celtic's Owen Archdeacon had a shocker in the league game and he started the Final looking so nervy.

He wasn't helped by Cammy - the king of the one-liners - who sidled up, patted him on the head and said: "Don't worry, son, just play the way you did the last time and you'll be alright!"

I was yards away from that and I doubled over laughing. Cruel humour.

RANGERS: Woods, Nicholl, Munro, Fraser, Dawson, Butcher, D. Ferguson, McMinn, McCoist, Durrant, Cooper. Subs: MacFarlane, Fleck.

CELTIC: Bonner, Grant, MacLeod, Aitken, Whyte, McGhee, McClair, P. McStay, Johnston, Shepherd, McInally. Subs: Archdeacon, W. McStay.

DATELINE: Premier League: Ibrox, October 17, 1987:
Rangers 2 Celtic 2

I'VE read the Game of Hate headlines and shrugged my shoulders before, believing it was all hype. But this was one day when I genuinely feared a RIOT.

I was walking in fear on the park, scared stiff of what would happen next. It was a sour fixture and that was down to the ref.

Jim Duncan was under pressure from those supervisors in the stand and he lost the plot. He was a condemned man afterwards and never really took charge of a big game again.

That game cost too many people too much.

Chris Woods went to catch a cross and Frank McAvennie steamed in late to spark Terry Butcher and Graham Roberts into the fray.

Eleven years later I'd challenge you to watch the video of that match. If you look at the incident it's handbags at ten paces but before you knew it there were three players sent off. Only Robbo escaped punishment and he was probably the most guilty!

Next morning we were picking up the papers and seeing that there would be court action and I couldn't believe it.

What the hell does the Procurator Fiscal have to do with football?

That day cost Chris and Terry Skol Cup Final places against Aberdeen because they were banned and big Butch was never to play in another Final for the club. That wasn't justice for what happened.

Robbo, meanwhile, almost started a riot himself by conducting the choir singing The Sash. Amid all this mayhem, there was Graham with the gloves on waving his arms like he was in charge of Luciano Pavarotti at the Albert Hall. I have to say I laughed at the madness of it all.

We took a battering in that second-half, the nine men, and we should have been out of it when Billy Stark hit the bar.

But then I got a chance to set off up the right and go past Anton Rogan, the first cross was blocked but the second fell for Goughie and he toe-poked it home.

Two things stick in my mind from that split-second of elation, the venom that poured out of the Celtic fans and the noise that greeted the equaliser. It was like an aeroplane taking off.

I was lying exhausted on the ground in sheer joy and then I remembered I was in front of the Celtic end and I got up and left a bit sharpish!

RANGERS: Woods, Gough, Phillips, Roberts, D. Ferguson, Butcher, Francis, Falco, McCoist, Durrant, McGregor. Subs: Cohen, Cooper.

CELTIC: McKnight, Morris, Whyte, Aitken, McCarthy, Grant, Stark, P. McStay, McAvennie, Walker, Burns. Subs: Rogan, Archdeacon.

DATELINE: Tennents Scottish Cup semi. Hampden, March 31, 1992:
Celtic 0 Rangers 1

BEATING Celtic is sweet enough, beating them to make the Cup Final when you've played for 84 minutes in teeming rain with 10 men defies belief.

David Robertson's red card for clattering into Joe Miller was an Andrew Waddell shocker but I think the Gaffer hit the nail on the head when we came in soaked but smiling after Ally's goal clinched a dramatic win.

We fought for every single ball, got some breaks and played with pride in the jerseys.

The dressing-room after games like that is bizarre. Walter was trying to gather all the players together to tell us how proud he was of us and we were trying to arrange the night out!

You are oblivious to everything around you at times like that, running on adrenalin and no-one can get a word in edgeways for the shouting.

Eventually Walter shut everyone up and stood in the middle of the room with piles of soaking kit about his feet. For once there was silence and he said: "You've just shown everyone the TRUE Rangers."

He was right.

CELTIC: Marshall, Morris, Boyd, O'Neil, Mowbray, Whyte, Miller, McStay, Creaney, Nicholas, Collins, Subs: Galloway, Coyne.

RANGERS: Goram, Stevens, Robertson, Gough, Spackman, Brown, Gordon, McCall, McCoist, Durrant, Huistra. Subs: Rideout, Spencer.

DATELINE: Premier League Ibrox, August 22, 1992:
Rangers 1 Celtic 1

THIS game shows you how quickly your fortunes can turn on their head in football, because I remember being dejected that I was on the bench.

Trevor Steven had come back from Marseille and the Gaffer decided to go with him leaving me a frustrated sub - but I got my moment alright.

Still I'd got used to spectating when I was out injured and players like Trev made it easier to watch games. If there are two players I wish I'd played more with then they are Steven and Laudrup.

Trevor's move to France and injuries to both of us killed the first option and Lauders arrived at a time when I've been out of the picture a lot.

Trev also reminded of myself because even though he had this great partnership wide on the right with Gary Stevens deep down he was like

111

every midfielder with self-belief. He wanted to be in the middle, the No.10, the playmaker. The Guv'nor!

When he was given the chance he showed just what a good player he is and he'll be remembered I think as a great servant to Rangers.

We were down to a Gerry Creaney goal in this one when Pieter Huistra burst down the left and Mark Hateley unselfishly laid it back to me.

It was one of those moments you rarely get in an Old Firm game - time and space inside the box - and I arrowed a right foot shot into the top corner away from Gordon Marshall. As always the Enclosure boys got first sight of the Durranty smile. After all, it was my first Old Firm goal for SIX YEARS!

RANGERS: Goram, I. Ferguson, Robertson, Gough, McPherson, Brown, Steven, McCall, McCoist, Hateley, Huistra. Subs: Durrant and Mikhailitchenko.

CELTIC: Marshall, Boyd, Galloway, Grant, Mowbray, McNally, Miller, McStay, Creaney, Payton, Collins. Subs: Slater, O'Neil.

DATELINE: Premier League Celtic Park, November 7, 1992:
Celtic 0 Rangers 1

GOD, by now they must have hated the sight of us!

For me this was a win against all the odds again. We managed to keep 11 on the park this time but to be honest we had the worst preparation for an Old Firm game ever.

We'd triumphed in the European Cup Battle of Britain classic over Leeds United at Elland Road on the Wednesday night and then Stuart McCall and I had enjoyed some champers into the early hours.

But the business head was well and truly screwed back on come Saturday and Andy Goram was once again in the form that will make him an Ibrox legend.

They hit us with everything that day but Andy made mind-boggling saves from a Dariusz Wdowczyk free-kick and a Stuart Slater volley. Slater took so much stick at Celts but he had great skills and he showed them all that day - it still wasn't enough.

Another Andy stop from Gary Gillespie broke their hearts and my goal proved to be the winner.

I think to this day that McCoist must still have been under the influence of the bubbly because he actually knocked down Dale Gordon's cross instead of taking a touch and shooting himself.

I'd made a couple of runs off John Collins before that and he didn't match me and this time it paid off as I steered home Ally's header with my left foot.

I loved the tussles with Collins. He was one of the best I played against in Old Firm games and he scored some memorable free-kicks against us.

He's a class act and it doesn't surprise me that he has made it at Monaco. The coach there, Jean Tigana, is every midfielder's dream.

I always loved watching that French midfield of Tigana, Michel Platini, Alain Giresse and Luis Fernandez that won them Euro 84. They had everything.

I'd have loved to have gone somewhere like that under a coach like Tigana to see what I could do but it didn't happen. I always knew that if John clinched his ticket he'd be a success.

CELTIC: Bonner, Galloway, Wdowczyk, Grant, Mowbray, Gillespie, Boyd, P. McStay, Slater, Creaney, Collins: Subs: Nicholas, O'Neil.

RANGERS: Goram, McCall, Robertson, Gough, McPherson, Brown, Gordon, I. Ferguson, McCoist, Hateley, Durrant. Subs: Huistra, Mikhailitchenko.

DATELINE: League Cup semi-final, Ibrox, September 22, 1993: Celtic 0 Rangers 1

THIS was one of the few times when you could ever say Ibrox was a NEUTRAL venue for an Old Firm match.

What an incredible atmosphere there was that night because it was a League Cup semi-final and the stadium was split 50-50.

We walked out to a sea of GREEN in front of us because Celtic had the Govan Stand as well as their traditional Broomloan Road End.

It was wall-to-wall passion and once more we had the bottle for the battle to win with ten men.

Pieter Huistra - who wasn't exactly the Chopper Harris of his generation - lost the place and kicked Tom Boyd up the backside to get sent off. Looking back it was funny but I wasn't laughing at the time.

When the chips are down in games like that then one little thing, one snap decision can sway the game your way.

I'd always remembered that inside the game Mike Galloway was known as a defender who liked to take risks. If there was a chance to play his way out he'd do it instead of pulling on the Adidas Standfinders and hitting Row X.

Well, that night he'd already dummied somebody out of it on the right wing but he wasn't going to fool me. I chased a lost cause and sure enough he tried to fake me and I didn't buy it. One sly little tug of the jersey, he'd been robbed and I was away to cut it back for Hateley to score. Ten out of 10 for us again.

CELTIC: Bonner, Boyd, Wdowczyk, Grant, McNally, Galloway, McGinlay, McStay, McAvennie, Creaney, Slater. subs: O,Neil, Mowbray GK: Marshall.

RANGERS: Maxwell, Stevens, Robertson, Gough, McPherson, McCall, Steven, I. Ferguson, Durrant, Hateley, Huistra. Subs: Wishart, Morrow GK: Scott.

DATELINE: Premier League Celtic Park, January 1, 1994:
Celtic 2 Rangers 4

I'VE spoken about the game when I was on the park and I felt a riot rumbling towards me.

Well, this was the day I feared I'd be caught up in a war with Celtic fans fighting each other.

Their punters felt the old board at Parkhead had dragged the club down and this was the day it all hit rock bottom.

I was injured and watched from the Gers bench as we raced into a 3-0 lead early on with Mikhailitchenko, who scored twice, sensational.

All sorts of crazy stuff was happening as the fans pitched missiles - anything from pie cartons to Mars bars - at the Celtic directors and the atmosphere turned worryingly ugly.

The cries of "Sack the Board" were deafening and the place felt as if it was going to erupt.

We went back to the safety of the dressing-room afterwards and you could hear the police vans racing everywhere as the trouble and fighting kicked off outside the ground.

The Celtic fans went over the edge that day but perhaps that was the day their club went so low that they had to climb back up.

CELTIC: Bonner, Gillespie, Boyd, Grant, Wdowczyk, McGinlay, Byrne, P. McStay, O'Neil, Nicholas, Collins. Subs: McNally, Biggins.

RANGERS: Maxwell, Stevens, Murray, Gough, Pressley, Brown, Steven, McCall, Durie, Hateley, Mikhailitchenko. Subs: Huistra, Kuznetsov.

DATELINE: Premier League Hampden, May 7, 1995:
Celtic 3 Rangers 0

THIS was the worst, the pits. Defeat is one thing but losing like this was a disgrace.

To make matters worse I was **CAPTAIN** for the second-half because John Brown went off injured.

It makes no difference to me that we struggled to get a team out that day. It hurts even now that I wasn't just a part of this, I had the armband.

It was 0-0 when Bomber limped away and we lost three after the break including a horrific Craig Moore own goal.

Pierre van Hooijdonk inspired them and I have to say he was one player I was glad to see the back of when he went to Nottingham Forest.

His fall-out with Fergus McCann was a blessing for Rangers because he was nothing but problems.

He's quality, a big-time player who loves the big atmosphere and I'm sure after the first season he's had at Forest he'll get back on to the stage he deserves in the Premiership.

For us, though, Pierre or no Pierre that day was unacceptable. The league was won and we had all heard Gazza was on his way from Lazio but I still couldn't stomach that performance. It was sickening, we let the club and the fans down.

CELTIC: Bonner, Boyd, McKinlay, Vata, O'Neil, Grant, McLaughlin, McStay, Van Hooijdonk, Donnelly, Collins. Subs: Falconer, O'Donnell.

RANGERS: Thomson, Moore, Cleland, Boli, McLaren, Brown, Steven, I. Ferguson, Durrant, Hateley, Laudrup. Subs: Mikhailitchenko, Murray.

That's a low note to finish the journey of my best and worst Old Firm experiences on - but I still had the Nine-in-a-Row game after that! These games have been like a drug to me with at least four fixes a season.

Now I'll watch a new era dawn as Dick Advocaat takes on Wim Jansen next season. I hope Dick brings success to Rangers and emulates the job Wim has done at Celtic. Jansen has been brilliant for them.

Tommy Burns is a person, a player and a manager I have massive respect for. Things never worked out for him in charge of Celtic but he set out a five-year programme and then was only given three years to turn things round.

I think he left a great inheritance for Jansen but after losing men I rated so highly like Paolo di Canio and Jorge Cadete what Wim has achieved has been marvellous.

Now it's all over for me in Old Firm games I can reflect on the fixture and I feel the spite isn't what it once was, there's more hatred at Pittodrie for a Rangers player than there is in the Celtic match now. I mean you're talking about a ground where Mark Hateley was attacked in the car park after a game and a set of fans who disrupted a minute's silence for Rangers' legend George Young. They hate us.

In Old Firm games now it has to be remembered they've taken the Jungle away at Parkhead and they've seated the Enclosure at Ibrox. For a traditionalist like me that's been a bodyblow.

Those areas are where the real Celtic and Rangers diehards stood and they created the atmosphere of the games all on their own. Any Rangers player is lying if he says the Jungle didn't intimidate him and as long as I live I'll never forget the sight of our East Enclosure in full cry.

Those days are gone now but at Pittodrie you're still very close to the fans and there is real nastiness there that dates back to the Alex Ferguson days, before that Neil Simpson tackle that cost me so much.

My days in those arenas are numbered but there's one place Ian Durrant will always have a seat. Ibrox.

I have four season tickets in the East Enclosure and that's where I'll watch my Old Firm games from now on. Wait a minute, maybe I'm a yuppie now that I've had a testimonial and an autobiography.

Reckon I should switch to the Main Stand? Nah, me neither.

I think I'll stick to my roots.

CHAPTER 11

LOST HORIZONS

IAN DURRANT and close pal Derek Ferguson stood on the Hampden sidelines clutching the Skol Cup in 1986 after they had crafted a dramatic 2-1 win over arch-rivals Celtic.

Boss Graeme Souness predicted they would grace the national stadium for years to come in the dark blue of their country but they will end their careers with just 13 caps between them.

Injury cost the country two talents they could ill afford to lose but Durrant has emerged with some sparkling memories of an international career that should have left his portrait hanging in the SFA Hall of Fame.

Here he reflects on what might have been and the greats he did face in a Scotland stint tragically wrecked by that crippling injury.

MADRID, Spain. we're outside the Bernabeu one night in April 1988 and I'm cowering on the floor of the Scotland team-bus as bricks rain through our windows.

International football, Lesson No.1 - the locals don't like it when you frustrate their heroes and come away with a 0-0 draw.

That night of defensive heroics was one of my 11 caps. Doesn't seem much to look back on, but every Scotland game was an adventure and Madrid was one that will always live with me.

What a place the legendary home of Real is - so intimidating. There were only 35,000 scattered around the massive tiers that night, but that was enough.

You could feel the hostility from the minute we walked out - yet I have to say I loved the place. The surface was superb and if you're a player at all you pray for the chance to play against the likes of Michel.

He was at his peak then and it was a fantastic challenge but one that could only make me better.

There was no time to reflect on it afterwards, though, because the local fans lost the plot and a horde of them attacked my old boss Jock Wallace and Jock Brown - then a commentator instead of Celtic's General Manager - outside the ground.

Jock Brown would have **TALKED** them to death, but The Gaffer had a cut under his eye and being the old jungle fighter he was raging.

Missiles from a mob began pelting the bus and while everyone else was diving for cover he was hollering: "Let me get a hit at one of them."

Then a huge brick came crashing through the window just missing Maurice Johnston's head and we all dived to the deck.

There was an enormous hole in the glass and then from scrambling about the floor in terror I was on the ground laughing when Coisty shouted: "Mo, pop your head up and see if they're away."

International football at its best and something I didn't get enough of - especially as at the time I was in the reserves with Rangers after Souness kicked me out of the top team.

I'd been labelled unprofessional because trouble was following me around. The latest blot on my landscape came when I was accused of being part of a brawl outside Panama Jax disco in Glasgow.

It was hanging over me and things weren't so clever. I was a hothead and I went into Graeme's office and as the words started flying we both over-reacted.

When I look back he was trying to look after me but I felt he was picking on me. I would be out of the first team for a month. He said to me: "I'm not playing you. I'm not satisfied with your attitude."

I said: "Well, if you're not playing me I'll go somewhere else and play."

He said: "Go on then, I'll phone you later."

118

I had resigned myself to leaving Rangers but I had no agent, the only way I ever heard of a team being in for me was reading that there was interest from the likes of Fiorentina in the paper.

I was cleared of any involvement in that fight in the end but Scotland was an escape back then and Andy Roxburgh's faith in me meant a lot.

I'd played for my country at every level as a kid and I was edging towards full recognition from the night I outplayed Gazza in the Under-21s at Pittodrie.

We talk about that Scotland-England game to this day and Paul knows I got the better of him with Derek Ferguson and Peter Grant alongside me - even though they won 1-0.

They had Gascoigne, their goalscorer Michael Thomas and an overage player called Stewart Robson who was at Arsenal.

But I did well and by the time the second leg came around at Craven Cottage, we lost out, I was in Roxburgh's national squad.

It all started for me on September 9, 1987 at Hampden at the age of just 20 when Roxy gave me my debut in a friendly against Hungary.

It was a familiar story that night as I set both goals up for McCoist but it was an evening that meant a lot because my dad was still alive then.

He saw me play for Rangers and Scotland and at least I have that to comfort me when I think of him now.

I remember the week of that game seeming to pass in a flash because the newspapers all wanted to speak to me. I was the new kid on the block and I suppose the attention would be the same now if a kid that age made it through.

Back then I was naive as hell. Sure, I'd been away with Rangers but with Scotland we went away to The Gleneagles Hotel which was very swish for a wee boy from Kinning Park.

I wasn't happy with the food. We didn't have much nouvelle cuisine or pasta or fruit where I came from. So I sneaked up to the room and ordered two cheeseburgers for myself and I was so hungry I left the room door open as I raced in to eat them.

Roxburgh walked in and I had one of them half stuffed in my face. He's called me the Cheeseburger Kid ever since!

I needed my energy, though, because I had to run around after old Coisty making his tea and getting his newspapers.

Roxy's reign as Scotland boss has always been surrounded in controversy after the bust-ups he had with Richard Gough that eventually led to the skipper quitting international football.

Andy believed in the card-games and quizzes for the squad and he was slaughtered for it. Goughie, for one, has his own way of preparing and he **HATED** all that. He has told people that in no uncertain terms.

But I could always see the idea behind it even if senior pros found it tiresome. It was designed to build togetherness. When you're on a trip with Scotland you're away for a long time and it drags.

You're watching other teams, studying videos and all you want is the day of the game to come round.

Roxburgh and Craig Brown try to fill that time and although they are called schoolmasters, look at their records with Scotland. They don't need to explain themselves or their methods to anyone.

Bottom line is Andy liked me and included me in every one of his teams until I was injured.

That took me in against the best in the world and I won't join the queue to slag him off. Roxy treated me well and I respect him.

I only worked under Craig for two games - a defeat in Italy and a win over Malta - and that wasn't long enough for me to make a personal judgement.

But if you want to ask how good he is, go to my Ibrox team-mate Jocky Bjorklund. Sweden will be on the beach instead of at France 98 with us and that's down to Craig in a big way.

Rangers and Scotland has been a prickly issue since the Souness era with all sorts of accusations levelled over our guys pulling out of squads.

But I don't agree that Souness dragged people out unnecessarily. Look around at SFA HQ and you'll see Graeme up there in the Hall of Fame. He's patriotic, no question.

He is, however, also a realist. He protected the club's investments if the players had an injury and they had an international looming.

It's an accolade playing for Scotland but when it comes down to the bare bones, the club pays your mortgage. They put the roof over your head and food in your family's mouths.

You can get injured with Scotland and lose your place in your club team and then you get slated from all quarters.

For all the stick the Gers players took at times I loved playing for Scotland because I felt my game was made for international football. I'll always feel that it was a benchmark for me.

For instance, I played against Italy at Ibrox in November 1992 and something Andy Roxburgh said struck me as one of the nicest football compliments I'd ever been paid.

The game came in the wake of the Battle of Britain European Cup clashes with Leeds and Andy said: "At Elland Road Ian Durrant brought some common sense to a hysterical football situation.

"He was always calm and composed in demanding situations and that's the sign of a very good player."

I took that on board against Italy as we drew 0-0 and I was up against AC Milan's Roberto Donadoni. What an experience.

Their team was studded with stars like Franco Baresi, Gianluigi

Lentini and Roberto Baggio. Baggio was without doubt the best player I have ever faced, closely followed by Michel from the Spanish side of 1988, and I had to swap jerseys with him.

Later I gave it to Tony, who owns an Italian restaurant in Bothwell called Da Luciano, and he looked like a Lottery winner!

What a team they had that night and yet we played brilliantly. The only pity was we could actually have beaten them.

Gordon Durie's workrate and bravery on a pitch never fails to amaze me but I was cursing it that night.

In this, my last season at Rangers, Jukey has collapsed on the Rugby Park pitch and scared the life out of us all when he was rushed to the Southern General.

Thankfully, he recovered but that was typical of him - taking the head knock and playing on. He did it at Ibrox against Italy and as a result he was concussed when we got the chance of the match and I was out in front of an open goal. He shot!

I couldn't believe it. I was playing for Scotland from the start for the first time in four years and I'd had my chance of the winner against Italy. Now it was gone.

I was calling him all the greedy bastards under the sun but I broke his heart in the return.

When we met them in Rome in October 1993 with Craig in charge as caretaker boss, the irony was that I cheated Gordon out of a goal.

We were 2-1 down and I got in the way of a shot from Jukey to stop us equalising. You know, Baggio was brilliant in Rome in the unforgettable Olympic Stadium yet at Ibrox Alan McLaren marked him out of the match. He was a prince, though, a superb player. He glided into angles and was always available for the ball. I'd love to have played with him.

He could certainly teach Lentini how to be a player. I mean, £13m? He played more like a bowl of Lentils that night at Ibrox.

Still, you couldn't argue with their style. That night our Umbro kit stank as if it had been packed away for weeks. The Italians? They smelled like they had just come from a beauty parlour and every one of them looked like a movie star.

I thought I had no chance of getting a jersey because they wouldn't want mine without a good wash!

It took me six years to earn 11 caps for Scotland. The injury made it bloody hard work. But I had good times and it made me understand just how good players at other clubs were.

Willie Miller and Alex McLeish, for example, had been foes at Aberdeen - but when you worked with them you realised they were made for the phrase battle-hardened.

My personal favourite, though, was Celtic captain Paul McStay. Class.

He never gave the ball away and I always loved players like that.

I always remember the furore of Rangers' alleged move for McStay but I honestly never heard talk of that.

I did believe the dressing-room chat that we'd offered to **DOUBLE** John Collins' wages when he left Hibs for Celtic. JC knocked it back because he had already shaken hands on a deal with Billy McNeill and the rest as they say is history.

He's gone on to grab a few vital goals for Scotland and I must confess it's always irked me that I never scored for my nation. It's a regret because I had my chances.

I almost got one on my debut in a World Cup qualifier against Norway in 1988 when we won 2-1.

The worst, though, was Malta in a 2-0 win in November 1993 that was to prove my last cap.

I was clean through on the keeper once and by the end I should have had a hat-trick. It just wasn't to be.

It was to be my finale for Scotland and there was a glut of midfield players around at the time like Gary McAllister, Ian Ferguson, John Collins, Billy McKinlay and Stuart McCall.

I faded out of the picture but the memories are there in the locker from Madrid to Rome, Malta to Oslo with a sackful of laughs in between.

We were always playing tricks on each other - traditionally Mo Johnston and Roy Aitken v Durrant and McCoist. My speciality is the breakfast of kippers and prunes to your rivals' rooms at 6am!

In Switzerland in September 1992 I'd be at the centre of two stories that still make me smile. First Roy Hodgson, the then-Swiss boss who is now at Blackburn, asked for a special dossier on me because I'd been out of international football so long with the injury he didn't know who I was!

Then Duncan Ferguson lost a brain cell and topped the lot. We'd lost 3-1 but been allowed a couple of drinks afterwards and Dunc was the scapegoat. He was the butt of our jokes all night. We annihilated him.

But he got his revenge when he **BARRICADED** Ally and I into our room. Every piece of furniture was piled against our door - even a **PIANO**! We got up at 8am and panicked when we couldn't get out.

Derek Whyte told me afterwards that Dunc was standing by this Wall of Jericho of furniture trying to get a lighter to fire up until he hauled him away. Thank God he did - because we'd never have got out.

Believe it or not, there were bars on the window of the room!

Not one of Dunc's better ideas, but we could still laugh about it later. Honest! Still, if that was the night a team laughed together, I also played the night a team died.

Lisbon's Stadium of Light on April 28, 1993 was a bridge too far for too many of us in what had been an exhausting and glorious season.

Rangers had won the Treble and gone so close to the European Cup Final. Goughie never played for Scotland again after that night against a side inspired by Jorge Cadete, who'd later come to Celtic.

It was a complete disaster.

I came on as a sub when we were 5-0 down and watched in horror as Coisty broke his leg in a challenge with Oceano.

He had scored 49 goals in all competitions that season and would have sailed through the half century and on to even more records. Yet it all ended in an instant, a bone snapped and he was out for almost a year.

I knew how he felt. Empty.

Portugal had Cadete, Fernando Couto, Paolo Futre - who had a stormer - and a surprise choice in a little guy called Rui Barros who destroyed us.

Roxburgh's famous quote was: "A team died out there".

And he was right. The dressing-room was silent afterwards. Andy walked around stunned as medical staff flew back and forth trying to get Coisty settled.

It was a very subdued journey, then the rebuilding started. I couldn't even talk to Ally - he was in a lot of pain and had a row of seats all to himself to keep the leg straight out.

The ambulance came to the airport to take him to Ross Hall and I went to visit him next day. The sparkle was gone, he was heartbroken.

I look back at those Scotland days with a big slice of sadness and regret in some ways because I honestly believe that if I'd stayed fit then, like Ally, I would have made the Hall of Fame.

I was only beaten three times in those 11 games for Scotland, a record I'm proud of - yet I only scratched the surface as an international player.

But I couldn't expect more, really. I was a regular before the injury and after it when I was hitting a peak again they recalled me.

The rest of the time I haven't been playing regularly enough for Rangers to be considered for Scotland.

It hurts I never played more often but I've played for the club I dreamed of and represented my country at every level.

I can live with that.

DURRANT: THE SCOTLAND STORY

Fr September 9, 1987: Scotland 2 Hungary 0 (McCoist 2)
EC October 14, 1987: Scotland 2 Belgium 0 (McStay, McCoist)

Fr March 22, 1988: Malta 1 Scotland 1 (Sharp)
Fr April 27, 1988: Spain 0 Scotland 0
WC September 14, 1988: Norway 1 Scotland 2 (McStay, Johnston)

WC September 9, 1992: Switzerland 3 Scotland 1 (McCoist)
WC October 14, 1992: Scotland 0 Portugal 0
WC November 18, 1992: Scotland 0 Italy 0

WC April 28, 1993: Portugal 5 Scotland 0
WC October 13, 1993: Italy 3 Scotland 1 (Gallacher)
WC November 17, 1993: Malta 0 Scotland 2 (McKinlay, Hendry)

* KEY: Fr (Friendly) WC (World Cup qualifier) EC (European Championship qualifier)

CHAPTER 12

FANTASY FOOTBALL

IAN DURRANT the manager, Ally McCoist as his right-hand man and a new Ibrox regime where players are fined for staying in!

That's what is ahead of the Gers stars if the deadly duo ever get their ultimate wish and take over the reins.

Until that unlikely day Ian has to content himself with an episode of Fantasy Football.

This is the chapter of Blue and White Dynamite that he dreamed up, he'd whiled away hours on team buses picking the teams in his mind.

Now is your chance to pick an argument as Ian selects his Dream Teams from his 14 years as an Ibrox idol - a Graeme Souness Select against the Walter Smith XI.

WHEN we sat down to write this book I always had one chapter that I was desperate to do and this is it.

I've loved over the years pondering just who would be in my all-time Rangers Dream Team.

Now I've got the chance and I've changed the script by having two teams. I've even resisted the temptation to pick myself because I'm the manager of both sides.

I consider myself lucky to have played beside the men I've named in the Souness Select and the Smith XI and I've got no doubt my teams will cause a thousand pub arguments.

Still, one thing's for sure. If we ever lost there would have to be a Sunday afternoon inquest - held over a quiet drink in the Cricklewood Hotel in Bothwell of course!

My first team is picked from the Souness revolution, five trophy-laden years under a manager who changed the club forever.

THE SOUNESS SELECT

(4-3-3)

CHRIS WOODS

GARY STEVENS   TERRY BUTCHER   RICHARD GOUGH   JOHN BROWN

DEREK FERGUSON   GRAEME SOUNESS   RAY WILKINS

ROBERT FLECK   ALLY McCOIST   DAVIE COOPER

SUBSTITUTES: MARK WALTERS and STUART MUNRO

CHRIS WOODS was the best in Britain when he came to Rangers and a tremendous lad too.

I thought he would be impossible to replace but in fact in Andy Goram we were to get an even **BETTER** keeper. The Goalie has surpassed everyone for me.

Woodsy's parting from the club when he eventually left for Sheffield Wednesday was messy. Yet I always felt Chris dug a hole for himself when paper talk started appearing saying he fancied a move back to England.

But he was a superb keeper whose class was shown in that constant battle for the England jersey with the legendary Peter Shilton.

126

GARY STEVENS wasn't the most gifted player but what an engine he had. He was a defender first and foremost and one of the best.

He made that right-back position his own like no-one has since.

RICHARD GOUGH has great positional sense and the experience to read situations so well, then the class to mop up the danger. He's an inspirational leader.   .

TERRY BUTCHER simply had presence beyond belief at the heart of a defence yet his skills were very under-rated. I called him the Winchester because he could pick you out from anywhere and rifle a 60-yard ball with that trusty left peg.

JOHN BROWN would never be out of my team. He had this frightening will to win and having been a midfielder he too was a great passer of the ball. My left-back is Mr Aggression and every team needs one.

DEREK FERGUSON would never forgive me if I left him out of the team but he deserves his place anyway.

Back in October 1986 when we played so well in the 2-1 Skol Cup Final win over Celtic we were tipped to be legends but injuries have haunted both of us.

I always thought Derek was going to be so special for Rangers but his shoulder became a constant worry and he had a lot of run-ins with Souness. It's a shame it never worked out because his passing ability is top drawer.

GRAEME SOUNESS was arrogance personified and I often wish we'd got him just two years earlier in his career. As I've said before forget Paul Ince, this man was the Guv'nor. I remember the New Year Old Firm game in his first season when he took possession in midfield and simply stood there feigning to pass but never actually touching the ball. He had four of them running all over the place before he got fed up and sprayed a ball out to Coop. Brilliant.

RAY WILKINS was The Wee General to me and he was awesome. You could count on the fingers of one hand the amount of times he gave the ball away during a game - sometimes he didn't give it away at all. I remember I was in the Ibrox sauna having a shave when he walked in and that was the first I knew he'd signed!

A lovely man and a great influence from the first time he walked into the Ibrox dressing-room and said: "Morning, chaps!" in that prim and proper London accent.

He had this cultured image but he loved a night out and was always up for a laugh - like writing "Shilts - England's No.1" on the inside of Woodsy's shinpads!

DAVIE COOPER is the most talented player I have ever seen and he only had one leg! It was unthinkable for Davie to actually use his right to kick the ball but who needed it when you had a left foot like his? Before me it was Bobby Russell who made all the runs for him but that telepathy just seemed to continue when I took over.

ROBERT FLECK was a great foil for Coisty in his prime and left Rangers too soon. Used his body well to keep defenders off him and was a good finisher who could be relied on for 20 goals a season.

ALLY McCOIST MBE is THE striker of his generation and a man I've loved playing beside. It's easy amongst all the jokes and the chat shows to forget just how good he has been for Rangers. Remember when the Golden Boot broke his leg in April 1993 he had scored 49 goals that season and there was still six weeks left.

That team would face a Smith XI that has some unsung heroes in it and guys I know can still play a massive part in the Rangers of the future.

THE SMITH XI
(3-5-2)

ANDY GORAM

CRAIG MOORE   RICHARD GOUGH   JOACHIM BJORKLUND

ALEX CLELAND   DAVID ROBERTSON

IAN FERGUSON   PAUL GASCOIGNE   STUART McCALL

MARK HATELEY   BRIAN LAUDRUP

SUBS: BARRY FERGUSON and CHARLIE MILLER

ANDY GORAM is the man with the dodgy knees, who flies through the air with the greatest of ease. Ladies and gentlemen...I give you The Flying Hippo!
He made a save from Pierre van Hooijdonk in the 3-3 Old Firm draw

that sums him up. Pierre flashed a ripping volley for the top of the rigging from about six yards and somehow the Hippo clawed it out from behind him.

It defied belief. But then Andy so often does.

ALEX CLELAND for me has had an unbelievable stint at Rangers since coming in that £750,000 deal that also brought Gary Bollan to us from Tannadice. He was regarded as a squad player but he's shown he's so much more than that.

CRAIG MOORE is a player who has been forced to play in a lot of positions for Rangers like right-back or midfield where he is not at his best. Fans judge him on that and it's wrong.

If you saw Skippy at centre-half then you'd realise just what he can contribute to the Gers in the future.

RICHARD GOUGH is in BOTH my Dream Teams and I think that shows you just what the Skipper has meant to us.

JOCKY BJORKLUND has this tremendous knack of timing last-ditch tackles that save you. I know his distribution can be wayward at times but as a stopper he's world class.

DAVID ROBERTSON was the mirror image of Gary Stevens at his peak but on the left flank - and there is truly a gap that has never been filled. He was excellent going forward and has pace to burn, he also scored a lot of goals from there and that's a vital help in the modern game when defences are hard to break down.

STUART McCALL was in my All-Time Eleven any time I sat down and tried to work it out. I call him Tony the Tiger because he's always in there fighting for possession and he's great to play beside.

PAUL GASCOIGNE scored the hat-trick in the 3-1 win over Aberdeen that won eight-in-a-row and walked into Ibrox legend. Those two solo goals that day were above anything I've seen, I was on the bench and they were actually thinking of bringing Gazza off. Then he did that.

IAN FERGUSON is a member of the elite Nine-in-a-Row club with those successive title medals and an excellent, committed Ranger.

Sure, he's combative but he's also a great passer of the ball with a real eye for the goal. Who could forget that brilliant scissors kick in the 3-2 Skol Cup Final win over Aberdeen in 1988?

I was only two weeks out of my first knee op then and almost injured myself again celebrating Fergie's strike.

MARK HATELEY was tagged Attila and he was as fearsome on the park as some of his suits were off it! I actually checked his locker one time because I felt sure he must have switched to Versace football boots.

BRIAN LAUDRUP has been called the finest ever player to wear a Rangers jersey. Well, he's second to Coop in my eyes but that still makes you a fair player!

One of my big regrets is that I have never played enough with him and I have always considered it a compliment that he told me he wished he'd been beside me more.

That's my dream teams and I have to say I'd take the Souness side to win simply because they have Coop playing for them.

It would be 1-1 until the dying stages then Davie would have screamed home a 30-yarder.

I've loved picking my teams for this book and it of course brings the question of whether I would like to be a coach when I finish playing.

Rangers have made me an offer of a post rearing the kids and I was honoured by it but never tempted. I still feel I have too much to offer as a player for now. As for managing Rangers one day Ally and I are deadly serious - but no-one believes us!

CHAPTER 13

A DAY IN THE LIFE

COME *with Durrant on his favourite journey ... through a Saturday playing for Rangers.*

From breakfast with his beloved son to the heavy metal music which pumps him up, his pre-match meal, the dressing room superstitions and the player who could sleep for Scotland.

The hours till kick-off which seem like years ... the scramble for spare tickets ... the laughs ... the anguish of those left out of the side.

Then the warm-up, the stretches, the smell of the liniment. And, finally, the roar of the crowd.

Durrant, who has played almost 350 times for the club he loves, takes you on the best part of the journey for any player - but especially one who dreamed of playing for his local heroes.

That walk down the tunnel. The first shafts of light. And then the buzz of 50,000 fans screaming your name.

He has only one word for it. Heaven.

MATCHDAY. This is what it is all about.

From the waking moment your eyes squint at their first chink of light, everything is geared to three o'clock.

Little has changed about my routine down the years - except the time I wake up. Max has seen to that.

Before he was born I'd lie on until 10.30, but these days I'm up playing with him by nine. I'm out of bed to put on his favourite Barney videos and let him run around the TV room before we have our cereal together.

When I was younger I used to wake up grumpy but that happens less now because I've got Max to look after.

If it's sunny I might stick on a pair of trainers and go out and test the surface on the back lawn.

We have mini-goals and a pile of old training balls out there for Max and I to play with and the wee man can pretend to be who he likes.

He's already Rangers-daft and he loves to wear his strip on a matchday. I look at him with his excellent Nike top with *Max 10* on the back and smile at the hand-me-down Rangers strips I used to have.

Some days Max will be Gazza, some days it's Goram, some days he even pretends to be his dad. He's bright for a two-year-old kid and I have to admit Gazza is his favourite. I can live with that.

I hope he grows up to be a footballer and he already has a fantastic left foot. Thankfully, he takes the good looks from Angela! He's a bundle of fun and now we have my little daughter Sophie who was born just as we completed this book - just in time for her dad to say how beautiful she is and give her a mention in his life story!

The kids mean the world to me and I feel I've matured a lot since Max was born and since I was married to Angela on June 4, 1994.

That day in Bothwell Parish Church was special to me and I'm lucky to have someone with her head screwed on behind me.

Football can be a treacherous business for marriages and you see a lot of break-ups but my missus knows the pitfalls and we're just getting stronger together.

She's my wife and my best friend too. I've had some tough times and she has always been there for me.

During the summer if I have five weeks off I dedicate every moment to the family and I love it. I look forward sometimes to the day when I retire because hopefully we will have enough money then to do a lot of travelling together.

I have phoned Angela from a lot of exotic - and not so exotic - places where I have been playing football and wished she was there. Then we'll be able to go back together. I look at Max these mornings and he reminds me of her with his blond hair. And I think again how lucky he is not to take after his old man.

When we've blown away the cobwebs I go back inside and have my shower and my shave, put on the club blazer, tie and trousers and head for the office. Ibrox.

Beards and moustaches used to be banned at Ibrox and then Souness came as manager and that went out the window.

But I've always shaved on the day of a game - it makes me feel fresh and ready to go. You'll never see me running out like Negri!

I've come a long way from that Ford Capri Red Devil with its furry dice that was once my pride and joy and these days we have a Mercedes and a Golf GTi in the driveway.

On matchdays I'll get in my Merc and head for Ibrox, planning to arrive there bang on noon.

And the build-up for the game starts then...with the music.

I like stuff that gets you pumped on matchdays, so I'll blast out *November Rain* by Guns and Roses, a revamped mix of Joy Division's *Love Will Tear Us Apart* or even *Pretty Vacant* by the Sex Pistols.

If Angela has been in the car you can be sure there will be a soul CD on but that usually gets slung out to make way for some noise.

I park on Edmiston Drive and even at noon there will always be a small knot of autograph hunters. I always stop for them because I used to be them. I was there, waiting behind that Albion wall to nick a ball or sneaking through a hole in the fence to see the Rangers. I know them.

Sometimes I get surprised that the inside of Ibrox is so fascinating to other people - but I forget that it's not their second home like it is mine.

That's the way the stadium is to me. I've been going in and out of there for the last 17 years. So let me take you on the Durrant guided tour through matchday.

When you walk through the big swing doors at the front, you're faced by the new security desk which is usually staffed by Peter the doorman.

His oval desk in the centre of the marble hallway is the hub of Ibrox where you pick up your fan mail - or hate mail - leave your car-keys or find your messages.

Then it's past him and up the famous staircase to the landing where I've walked a few times in trepidation - the Gaffer's office with all those imposing portraits of former bosses staring down is up there.

You might go in there for contract talks or to chap on his door and ask why you're not in the team but in general I've learned you very rarely come out of that room a winner.

It's a place to avoid on matchday, so I turn left into our little palace. The Players Lounge, the place where I feel at home.

The minute I go in the door the crack starts flying and I dish out abuse to the kitchen staff Tiny and Irene, asking them what crap is on today.

Not that it would ever matter. I eat the same thing before every game...a pint of milk and some chicken and beans.

But as you look about you'll see some bizarre diets in there now. Stuart McCall digging into his branflakes and bananas or Sergio Porrini with pasta and only oil on it - he's so fanatical about diet he won't even have a little sauce. That's bred into them at Juventus.

The girls know all our little foibles off by heart by now and even with all the foreigners they learn the new dishes quickly.

There are two long trestle tables in there and one at the far end and it's a special place, a football place.

We all sit across from each other and the patter will be flying as guys get up and down to refill their milk or juice from two whirring machines in the corner.

Football Focus comes on and I'll sit and slaughter Gary Lineker or tell Coisty he couldn't lace Lineker's boots on telly and he should chuck it.

As time ticks on the chatter becomes incessant. It's a nervous thing and it builds up as more players arrive. You pray for a race at 1.10 because that means you can use up some time sending one of the young boys to put a bet on at the bookies on the concourse.

After watching that you're starting to feel the adrenalin course through you and at 1.30pm it's like a signal that we're almost ready to go when Goughie walks in.

Guys like the skipper do things differently and he could sleep for Scotland. He'll kip until about 11am on a Saturday and then make his way in to the stadium.

He has breakfast at home and Tiny or Irene know that when he comes in he's only looking for a piece of toast and honey before he gets ready for another 90 minutes.

We come out of our lounge and back down that marble staircase to lay out our complimentary tickets. For me this always means a visit to Laura Tarbet, the Gaffer's secretary, who is a genius at finding spares.

Then it's into the dressing-room and you start to get ready. Even now after almost 350 first team games for the club there are still times when I look around in wonder and think back to the days on the terraces howling "Parlane, King of Ibrox" at the top of my voice.

Now here I am beside the Gorams, the Goughs and the Gazzas of this world. Wonderful.

As you come in the door you'll see the pegs of Gazza, McCall, Jocky Bjorklund and the Goalie.

Then over in the opposite corner you have the United Nations - Marco, Tony Vidmar - now the quietest man in the place after the departure of Erik Bo Andersen - Gordan Petric and Charlie Miller who is in there as India's entry because he eats so many curries.

Negri has fitted in very well because he has this lovely dry sense of humour and as his English improves he gets better and better.

It's funny for me seeing someone apart from Ally in the No.9 jersey but it's Marco's property now and he deserves it.

The Italians are always there on the days out and enjoy the banter of the club and Negri has asked McCoist for advice a lot. Ally is The King of Ibrox but he knows every king's reign ends some day.

Glance across to Ian Ferguson, one of the most superstitious players I have ever shared a dressing-room with. He will put one boot on before the other until we get beaten and then he changes the sequence. And, of course, the right side of his jersey must be hanging outside his shorts.

Then there is the Goalie. Now, Goram is at a disadvantage to start with because - as we all know - keepers are half-daft.

But if I glance towards him I see this tough guy footballer hanging up his lucky horseshoe, lucky teddy-bear and lucky chain on his peg.

On training days at Ibrox these days it has become a very crowded place. There are 31 players there now and Goughie often jokes with me that it looks like an American football locker-room.

In days gone by the younger lads like Charlie Miller, Derek McInnes and Rino Gattuso might have changed down in the away dressing-room but they've earned their slots in there now.

The squad is too big and I think Walter has known that throughout all of my last season but even if you're out of favour Ibrox is a very hard place to leave.

There's a mad corner in this special place and I'm at the heart of it with McCoist, Alan McLaren and Ian Ferguson. Standing in between us you have Jonas Thern and Peter van Vossen, the Bewildered Brothers, who look around them and wonder where they've landed.

Away from the banter just along from the dressing-room you'll find the gym which has become my domain since the injury. When you are as seriously hurt as I was you have to build up the muscles around your knee to help protect it.

That means working on your quads - the big muscles on the front of your thighs - and your hamstrings. And that, for me, means the King Kong Unit. It's a work-out devised for me by our physio Grant Downie and I do it three times a week.

It's a punishing power based exercise where you push yourself and your legs through 2,000 repetitions every week of your life.

I have slackness in my knee and so I also take on a device called a wobble-board where you seesaw back and forth and take the strain. You have to build up those other areas of your legs.

People say it must take discipline to keep doing it when other players without a history like mine can have a day off. But King Kong is just a part of my life now.

Sometimes when you go into the gym it's a struggle but the boogie box helps unless Ally is in there and he's torturing you with Bon Jovi every day of the week. I've started bringing in The Prodigy and stuff like that to vary it and to annoy the old man.

Back on matchday, it's nearing 2pm and the keepy-uppie game starts. This was Archie's idea – you all play and you're out if you miscontrol it.

Those games have always been a laugh but the heady-tennis is very competitive. Coisty and I are rubbish at that because we argue so much.

The kings are the Gaffer and Archie or Bomber and John McGregor and we all have to try and get to their heights.

Just after 2pm, Walter Smith gets to the part of the week that he must relish and we go once more through set-pieces, our corners and who we are to shadow when we are defending.

Those setpieces - attacking and defending - are pinned up on a board from 12noon onwards and all the players study what we are about. Then the boss names the team and by now hopefully I'm in and I am getting hyperactive. I'm always like this, a bundle of energy desperate to be released onto that pitch.

There's a corridor just off the dressing-room where you can go and get mats out to do stretching or you can go to the gym - either that or you're in that corridor with Gazza, battering a ball about.

Then at 2.30pm I pull on my favourite No.10 and get out that tunnel. You come down from the dressing room, burst into the light and hear the first chants from the East Enclosure.

I'll wave to my mum and Angela up in the Main Stand and then when the fans spot you're out the first chant goes up.

Then you pray that you have a day when you can keep them singing: "He's blue, he's white, he's ****ing dynamite, Ian Durrant, Ian Durrant."

Heaven really is a place on earth.

CHAPTER 14

LIFE WITHOUT RANGERS

LOSING. *Not a word many have associated with Rangers since the Souness Revolution in 1986.*

But now Ian Durrant must cope with loss, a life without the club he has lived and breathed since he first kicked a ball around under the yellow streetlights of Kinning Park.

Forget the spell at Everton, in his heart and in everyone else's eyes Durrant is a one-club man. Part of a dying breed.

His loyalty to Rangers is unquestioned but at 31 he knows it's time to go. Yet he knows that won't make the final parting any easier.

Here we find out how the fans' favourite feels he will survive.

A CAREER with Rangers is ending.

I've sat and wondered how people will remember me when I walk out of the club I love for a new challenge.

I hope there are those who will reflect on a special goal, a pass or something I did in a game that made it worth coming to watch.

But I know there are those who would rather paint me as some kind of George Best figure after all the "Durrant in Court" headlines years ago.

Listen, I am the first to admit that I did some daft things when I was young but it all seems a long time ago now. The truth is that things I did when I was naive and unable to handle the heat as a Rangers player have followed me through life.

Sadly, until people get to know you they can portray you as whatever they like. There is nothing I can do about that.

So I know what people will write about me and how some people will judge me even now.

I read those columns that slaughter you all the time, columns penned by writers that never have to face you at football grounds around Scotland.

I've read Tam Cowan in the Evening Times or Rikki Brown in The Sun having a real go at me and that's fair enough, they have a job to do and a boss to satisfy.

But I'd have more respect for them if they had the courage to stand up and face you when you're at a function or in a pub. Instead they scuttle away or exit out the back door.

Still, they're under pressure to dig that stuff up. There are two sides to any story, they're just not interested in hearing mine.

I admit it, I'm no angel. Never have been. But I honestly do feel the brushes with the law I've had are blown out of all proportion.

I was accused of hitting someone in that chip shop in East Kilbride when a guy was shouting the odds at me and I couldn't defend myself because I was on crutches. Coisty jumped in for me as pals do.

Second time around I was with Derek Ferguson, my pal Davie Currie and a couple of others when a crowd of people walked in to a kebab shop. I was standing there and the crack was fine until a girl said: "Simpson should have broken your other leg."

My mate didn't appreciate that and hit her in the face with a pizza and before I knew it I was charged with singing sectarian songs, which was bloody ludicrous.

The verdicts? The chip shop was Not Guilty and the kebab shop was Not Proven - so going by the justice meted out I'm hardly the hellraising yob I'm painted as.

The way it's constantly dug up bothered me at first. But now? I just laugh. After all, I *was* a bampot when I was a kid!

I have broken the rules and gone out on a Thursday night 48 hours before a game when I was younger because I was so naturally fit I could get away with it. Souness soon scared me out of that.

I made mistakes as a kid and went out when I shouldn't have. By my reckoning it must have cost me about £6,000 in fines and I lived to learn the lesson eventually.

Yet there is one thing that I will always bitterly regret and that's drink and drive on the day Graeme Souness quit Ibrox.

I hold my hands up to that and I fully deserved the 15-month ban and the £150 fine.

To be truthful with you I scared myself rigid, I was three times over the limit and it was the worst day of my life. You're labelled a drink-driver and once you fail the breath test and get to the police station the news goes round like wildfire.

Your self-esteem hits rock bottom because you're at a low point when you do something like that. I could have killed someone and I would never have forgiven myself.

I remember coming round the corner in my Ford Orion when I clipped the kerb and flipped the car on its roof. People thought I was out celebrating which if you know my regard for Souness from this book is far from the truth.

I was just a silly 24-year-old boy who had a lot to drink and thought he was OK to drive. I was naive and I paid the penalty.

But there are pressures that go with this great job of mine and I've lived with them for 14 years now. I need a break.

I saw the good it can do you to get away when Richard Gough came back from Kansas City Wizards and I noted how relaxed he was as a person and as a player. And, believe me, the skipper can be intense at the best of times.

Relaxed and Rangers just don't go together, though, it doesn't come with the territory.

And more than ever Richard has felt that this season as we have started to leak goals more than usual. The heat was put on him as the returning skipper to stop the rot.

It's been hard for him because he wasn't given the chance to settle in to the pace again whereas new players are given months. That's the demands of Rangers.

It's a goldfish-bowl existence both for yourself and your family off the park at times.

I've never been in the superstar bracket like Gazza - who is bothered every two seconds on the rare occasions we go out - but there are hassles that go with being a Rangers player in a football-mad city.

In Glasgow it's all they want to talk about from the works to the pubs, clubs and discos.

You're under scrutiny and I've learned to handle it now. I walk away from trouble.

The problem is that you will always be labelled in Scotland, that's the way our society is. And whether you play for Albion Rovers or Rangers you matter a lot to people here.

Now there is the appeal of moving somewhere where I can walk down the street without anyone asking me if I fancy a kebab!

I wouldn't exaggerate any pressure I have, though, because it has all been worth it.

I have made a good living from the game and I have played the guts of my career for the only club I ever wanted to join.

Now I face the crossroads and it's time to look up and take another route away from Ibrox. It's going to be a wrench.

I've been there for 14 years as a professional and two and a half years as an apprentice after leaving school early to sign an S form for Rangers.

But it's like everything else, there comes a time in your life when you must leave for pastures new.

I hope my testimonial doesn't prove to be my last game for Rangers at Ibrox because that would be a tear-jerker. I want to play in a league game after that and say farewell properly in competitive action.

Playing for Rangers is special, just ask guys like Ray Wilkins who has seen it all through Chelsea, Manchester United, England and AC Milan yet ended up in floods of tears when he went off the pitch after his last game against Dunfermline.

I respect Ray so much and he's told me to keep playing as long as I can which I want to do after all I've been through getting fit again from the knee injury.

Rangers were ready to offer me some sort of coaching position with the kids but while I was flattered it's too early for all that.

I have grown to hate Scottish football in some ways and I've fallen out with it because of the grind of playing each other at least four times a season.

You might line up against a team less than six weeks after you played them last and you know how they will line up.

I've always enjoyed European football more, always preferred that to the 100mph stuff.

If people reflect on my career I hope they'll look and say he dared to be different, even trying to slow things down and put my foot on the ball in an Old Firm game.

The one thing that really disappoints me is that there are nowhere near as many young players coming through as there were in my day.

The system now is such and the pace is such that if you played them you would burn them out. I've watched a lot of games in recent seasons and you don't really enjoy them because it is so frantic.

I pray for the likes of Charlie Miller and Barry Ferguson to make it. Barry reminds me of a young Ian Durrant and that's poignant as I get ready to leave.

I hope that under Dick Advocaat Charlie, Barry and Craig Moore are given their chance because they deserve it. I hope Advocaat brings that missing link of European success because the club is geared up for it but as I've said before he has a hard act to follow.

As for me who knows where I will go now? A better climate in the States or England and a place to take Angela and the kids on a new adventure?

I'd jump at the change of a change and wherever I go I won't carry the baggage of the reputation I have in Glasgow.

I've done alright. I come from a working class family who were happy to get out of Kinning Park for their holidays but I can give my own family privileges now and I'm proud of that.

My dad lived to see me play for the club he loved and for my country, my mum has seen all my games in a Light Blue jersey. I hope I've lived up to what they hoped from me.

And on a personal level I will walk out of Rangers as a player with my head held high and no regrets. I've had a great time.

I have worked under four great managers and now I honestly feel this is the dawn of a new era under Advocaat.

But it's also the close of a time that will surely go down as something special for the club. And those who follow us in the manager's office and the dressing-room have a lot to live up to.

Some fans and writers may have other feelings but I know that in my heart of hearts the 1993 Champions League side was for me the best team Rangers have **EVER** produced. I'm lucky to have been part of that.

Now I will be in tears the day it all ends, there is nothing surer. But at least I know that when my kids grow up I can tell them their old man played for the famous Glasgow Rangers.

I'm going and guys like Miller, Moore and McInnes must keep injecting the heart and the fun into the dressing-room, the way Coisty and I have for years.

There are strong characters leaving this club - from Gough and myself to perhaps McCoist and Goram. Those who follow must inherit the togetherness that Walter Smith has drummed into us.

The influx of foreign players and the language barrier is a problem in the Rangers of today, there's no avoiding that.

I've found that while we did everything together foreign players will at times do their own bit at training or whatever and leave.

Only time will tell if this is the right way to go. I hope so because the club is such a huge part of my life and I desperately want them to remain as successful as ever.

But I want a new lease of life now, to know that surge of enthusiasm once again.

As I leave, though, I hope the fans will always think of me as one of the boys - just a punter who became a player. And OK, I can't avoid it any longer. The question that keeps coming up as I ponder my future.

COULD I PLAY AGAINST RANGERS?

I'll be honest. It would be very difficult - but if someone else is willing to pay my wages then, yes, I would have to do it.

I've watched Coop with Motherwell and Wilkins with Hibs getting standing ovations when they returned to Ibrox and I'd like to think that would happen for me.

Those fans may find it strange if I ever came back wearing another club's colours. But they can be sure of one thing.

Ian Durrant's heart will always lie with Rangers.

THE END

Ian Durrant - Career stats

League	SCup	LCup	Europe
		1984-85	
5 (0)	0	0	0
		1985-86	
30 (2)	1 (1)	5 (0)	1 (0)
		1986-87	
39 (4)	1 (0)	5 (1)	5 (1)
		1987-88	
40 (10)	3 (2)	5 (3)	6 (1)
		1988-89	
8 (2)	0	4 (1)	2 (1)
		1989-90	
0	0	0	0
		1990-91	
4 (1)	0	0	0
		1991-92	
13 (0)	2 (0)	3 (1)	2 (0)
		1992-93	
30 (3)	3 (0)	5 (1)	9 (3)
		1993-94	
23 (0)	1 (0)	5 (1)	2 (1)
		1994-95	
26 (4)	1(0)	2 (0)	2 (0)
		1995-96	
15 (0)	3 (0)	2 (0)	6 (0)
		1996-97	
9 (0)	2 (0)	3 (0)	3 (1)
		1997-98	
5 (0)	1 (0)	1 (0)	1 (0)
		TOTAL	
247 (26)	18 (3)	40 (8)	39 (8)

Includes substitute appearances,
goals are in brackets

The statistics include matches up to 21 March 1998

First Team Debut
at Cappielow 20 April 1985
Rangers 3 v Morton 0

Ibrox Debut
27 April 1985
Rangers 3 v Hearts 1

First Goal
9 November 1985 v Celtic
in 3-0 victory at Ibrox

European Debut
2 October 1985 v Osasuna
(Away)

First European Goal
26 November 1986 v
Borussia Monchengladbach
(Away)

First Medal
League Cup Final v Celtic
October 1986
Scored opener in 2-1 victory

Summary Statistics
Played 344 matches and
scored 45 goals (excluding
friendlies and Glasgow
Cup ties)

Played in 7 Finals
(4 League Cup and
3 Scottish Cup) and won
every match.

Compiled by David Mason

IAN DURRANT

I would like to thank Kingy for all his hard work on this book and for at least paying for lunch a couple of times. I hope my mum Ruby enjoys it because I wouldn't have had a career at Rangers to look back on without her help and support.

To Ally McCoist MBE I would say thanks for the foreword and a lifetime of laughs and to Blair Morgan my agent keep negotiating.

To everyone at Rangers Football Club, you know you're in my heart wherever I go.

And, finally, to Angela and Max and Sophie. Thanks for being there.

IAIN KING

To Durranty, it's been a privilege. Thanks for the fun and for being on time for lunch - once.

Also thanks to the excellent staff at Sarti's for putting up with us.

To my dad Matt your support - and your bloody criticism - proved a great help again. Ally, respect for the foreword and thanks for getting me so drunk I then taped over every word you said.

Thanks go to the library staff at the Sunday Mail and my understanding Sports Editor George Cheyne for his backing.

Lastly, to Lorna thanks for keeping my life on track through another book and to Caitlin and Bruce thanks for the smiles.